Jack Finlay is sixty-two, and has been surfing, sailing and diving for most of his life. His articles and short stories have appeared over a lengthy period of time in Australian, and overseas, surfing, yachting and literary magazines. He is also the author of three books, *Bass Strait and Beyond*, *Caught Inside*, and *Fighters: 25 Australian Lives In and Out of the Ring*. Jack has been a member of Victorian surfing teams, is a former Victorian Veteran's Champion, and is still an active surfer. For six years he was the inaugural manager of the Surfworld Surfing Museum. He lives in Torquay, with his wife.

Wind on the Water

and other surf stories

Jack Finlay

Photography by
Jon Frank

Harper*Sports*
An imprint of HarperCollins*Publishers*

All characterisations in this book are fictional and any resemblance to persons living or dead is unintended.

Harper*Sports*
An imprint of HarperCollins*Publishers*, Australia

First published in Australia in 2006
by HarperCollins*Publishers* Australia Pty Limited
ABN 36 009 913 517
www.harpercollins.com.au

Copyright © Jack Finlay 2006

The right of Jack Finlay to be identified as the author of this work has been asserted by him under the *Copyright Amendment (Moral Rights) Act 2000*.

This work is copyright.
Apart from any use as permitted under the *Copyright Act 1968*, no part may be reproduced, copied, scanned, stored in a retrieval system, recorded or transmitted, in any form or by any means, without the prior written permission of the publisher.

HarperCollins*Publishers*
25 Ryde Road, Pymble, Sydney NSW 2073, Australia
31 View Road, Glenfield, Auckland 10, New Zealand
77–85 Fulham Palace Road, London W6 8JB, United Kingdom
2 Bloor Street East, 20th Floor, Toronto, Ontario M4W 1A8, Canada
10 East 53rd Street, New York NY 10022, USA

National Library of Australia Cataloguing-in-Publication data:

Finlay, Jack.
  Wind on the water.
  ISBN 13: 978 0 7322 8485 5.
  ISBN 10: 0 7322 8485 6.
  Surfing – Anecdotes 2. Surfers – Anecdotes I. Title.
797.32

Internal photographs copyright © Jon Frank except page i copyright © Chris Carey
Cover photograph: Andy Irons, with thanks to Billabong. Copyright © Scott Needham/SNP5000.com
Cover design: Louise McGeachie
Typeset in 11.5/16pt Goudy by Helen Beard, ECJ Australia Pty Ltd
Printed and bound in Australia by Griffin Press on 79gsm Bulky Paperback White

5 4 3 2 1   06 07 08 09

This book is for Sue, Erica and Carl, who rode these waves with me, and without whom I could never have made the drop.
It is also dedicated to anyone who has ever ridden a wave, and afterwards tried to express the experience.

Contents

Foreword	ix
Introduction	1
Tableau	5
The Day that Charlie Wilson Died	19
Fat City	31
Earth Journey	49
Food for the Soul	67
Time Traveller	83
Seasons	93
The Graduate	99
In the Red Corner	107
Jack the Wandering Albatross	115
Roadsong	121
Under the Awnings	133
Tube Ride	143
The Storm	151
The Low Road to Xanadu	165
Tattoo	173
Wind on the Water	181
Acknowledgments	199

Foreword

Surfing is just like the Catholic Church. It is so broad and diverse as to defy description, and it can touch everybody. But unlike the Church, surfing goes beyond the human species; dolphins, for example, surf with such grace and speed that a human surfer can only watch with admiration. Likewise the soar of an albatross, lifting and dropping across the face of a wave, inspired humans to completely change the way they surfed, and to reinvent the design of surfboards.

Surfing's breadth and diversity is apparent at its most fundamental level. When you're sitting out in the water, the person next to you may run a chain of porno shops, be a high court judge, a stoned mullet or an upwardly mobile executive. The ten-year-old kid catching a wave inside of you may surf better than you ever will. And yet there is something we all share: a love affair with the ocean. For some, it is even a fatal attraction.

Surfing also has its mystics: people whose connection to the ocean is beyond their control and our understanding;

whose vision is shaped more by the waves than the world in which they live and whose sense of self is in complete accord with the sea.

Kelly Slater, seven-time world champion and the most famous and commodified surfer in history, is also arguably surfing's greatest visionary and artist. He has done as much to chart the course of modern surfing as, for example, Jimmy Hendrix did in shaping the direction of contemporary music. Perhaps the only difference between a surfer, an artist and a mystic lies in their practice, in the way they choose to live it out.

Most of what the public knows about surfing has been designed to fit into a sports show on TV, or has been dumbed down and packaged so it can be bought and sold. But the truth is there are so many tales, and so many different perspectives, that you could fill a TV series like 'Australian Story' for the next millennium.

And that's where Jack Finlay comes in — he is a storyteller. He is also a sailor, a surfer and a boxer; almost a fair dinkum Jack-of-all-trades. It is these diverse threads that Jack weaves together. I believe this is what makes his stories unique. He takes us into many different worlds, for example in 'Fat City' we step into the boxing ring and it's only if we look closely, and to some degree we read between the lines, that we realise that the person telling us the story is actually a surfer. This is equally true of the narrator in 'Food for the Soul'. Not only are we looking through a surfer's eyes in these stories, but we are also witnessing a surfer's unique sensibility washing up against the ways of the world. It's here that we move beyond mere description and are invited to share in a cognitive process, a way of being.

Jack's stories take us past our preconceptions of surfing and allow us to see something deeper and far more elusive; a state where the mind has truly been shaped by the sea, and a response that can never be fixed but is like an ongoing dance in which we never know the next move.

When the stories deal directly with surfing and beach culture, the viewpoint is anything but set. We roam freely looking at everything with equally open eyes. Jack allows us to share in this experience; it is not simply described to us. The stories are an invitation into what has previously been a guarded and secret world.

Surfers are, by nature, guarded and secretive. If you discover buried treasure you are inclined to keep it secret, so others don't come and take it from you. So it is with surfing — to discover a good wave that no one knows about is a hard-earned prize indeed. This book provides a rare opportunity to share in this treasure.

Before Jack Finlay, I doubt that 'surfing' and 'boxing' ever appeared in the same sentence. For many, surfing is simply the best fun they have ever had — and that is reason enough to do it. But there is more to it than this. From its ancient Polynesian roots, surfing has always been a warrior culture. At the time of first white contact with Hawaii, everybody surfed. The general population lay on short wooden boards as they rode the waves to the beach. (These quite resembled the type of boards hired out on beaches up and down the east coast of Australia in the '30s, '40s and '50s.) But it was the King who could stand upright on a large wooden board and ride the ocean swell to the shore. His supreme power as warrior king was thereby demonstrated by his graceful and majestic mastery of the ocean.

Once the surf gets serious, once the waves are huge, it takes a warrior's heart to paddle out. Perhaps less obviously, it also takes rigorous training and discipline. Our first thought may be that surfers are free spirited and unfettered, and this of course is true. But for those who have given their life to surfing, much time is spent in preparation for challenges that will take them beyond all physical and mental limitations — challenges that are no less demanding than training for a heavyweight world-title bout. A 50-foot wave has enough power to light a city for a week! It will put you down as surely as if you had been king hit by Mike Tyson. On top of that you will probably drown! In both cases it is a rare type of person who will put their hand up.

To be allowed to share in this experience, from the safety of our armchair, is something for which we must all thank the author of this collection.

Simon Buttonshaw
Artist and surfer

'The sea never changes, and its works, for all the talk of men, are wrapped in mystery.'

Joseph Conrad

Introduction

In the western suburbs of Sydney one November Saturday morning, a twelve-year-old girl buys a T-shirt from a surf shop that is twenty kilometres from the ocean.

Some hours later, halfway across the world, a twenty-eight year old Hawaiian paddles a ten-foot board onto a wave the surf media will later describe as part of 'the first decent swell to hit Waimea Bay in years'. The image will later appear in the evening news bulletins of TV stations in thirty-four countries of the world.

That same night, back in Australia, an elderly diner at a beachfront restaurant in Torquay excuses himself from a table, and walks out into the moonlight to stand on a grassy verge overlooking the ocean. When he returns minutes later he is asked what he was doing. 'Checking the waves,' he says, and laughs. 'They've come up today.'

If, as the surveys tell us, there are millions of surfers worldwide, then it follows that there will always be just as many perceptions of what surfing is, and what it means to be a surfer.

For me, and I suspect a lot of other people, surfing has always had a lot more to it than just surfing.

I've always seen it as a spectrum; some part of it physical, a big part of it mental, an aspect that the stories in this book seek to explore. At one extreme is an expanse of open ocean over which the wind blows, imparting energy. At the other is a state of mind, and a way of seeing things. In between these two points is everything that is surfing, from the physical skills of catching a wave, through the vagaries of technology and fashion, to the intangibles of lifestyle, culture, art and attitude.

The stories in this book are surf and ocean swell stories, mainly fiction. The oldest of them was written (and published) in 1971, the most recent in 2005, and previously unpublished. They were written for a group I would call 'the true believers', surfers and lovers of the open ocean. Some of the stories, or forms of them, were first published in *Surfing World*, during the time when I was a regular contributor. Some also appeared in other sections of the surfing press, or in yachting, and literary magazines. Some of them helped form parts of the books *Bass Strait and Beyond*, *Caught Inside*, *Waves: Great Stories from the Surf*, and Jon Frank's photographic exploration, *Waves of the Sea*.

I wrote with several things to the forefront: a love of surfing, a belief in its largesse and liberation, and a conviction that it was truly a moveable feast that could travel with you through life, capable of embracing and accommodating all who came to it, no matter from which direction they arrived, or the manner in which they chose to do it. I never gave much weight to the surf industry's notions of 'cool'.

I wrote in the belief there were surfers out there interested in the experience of the imagination, for whom things didn't necessarily need to be spelt out literally, and for whom the written word could still create enduring images. Over time I tried to write about some of Australian and Victorian surfing's perennial themes — the country, 'down south', tube-riding, the seasons, travel and the never-ending highway, and so on.

Behind each theme, however, was the constant imperative of trying to express what it means to give over a fair degree of your life to the eternal energy of the ocean, and call yourself a surfer. Riding the waves is one part of it for sure, but standing alone, with a belief in yourself and the responsibility that goes with it, is another. The viewpoints will always be individual, and whether words or photographs, they are forever just the tip of an iceberg. This book's like that. Surfing's like that!

In the thirty-five year time-span over which these stories were written, a lot of things in surfing have changed — and yet nothing has changed!

Sure, the technology and equipment are now different, allowing almost impossible waves to be ridden with panache and style. Yes, a flourishing surf industry has finally arrived at its ultimate destination on Wall Street. As part of that same destination, communication technologies now beam the sport to hitherto undreamed-of audiences worldwide, at the same instant creating unlimited commercial potentials. And certainly the years have softened some of the historical peripherals in these stories.

But the spirit of surfing itself remains untouched.

That simple act of stroking onto a waveface and taking the drop, first begun in Polynesia all those years ago, remains as timeless as ever. Its promise and fulfilment, intimated at by Cook in Tahiti in 1777 as 'a most supreme pleasure', stands on offer as it always has.

The stories in this book were written to give expression to what the promise and fulfilment of surfing has always been, and still is, for me.

I hope you enjoy them, assembled here as one collection.

When you've read some of them, go out and go surfing! And keep surfing!

Jack Finlay
Torquay, 2006

Tableau

PROMISED LAND

Just before dusk, afte]r a long day's drive, I came upon the signpost and for no particular reason took the turn. I think that some half-remembered snatches of conversation from aeons past had carried the name. I can't be sure now, but whatever it was I knew I had stumbled onto something as the road began its descent to the coast, and through the trees I saw the faint but distinct lines of swell entering the bay.

A momentary dip and the sea was lost to sight. The road began a long last stretch into town, skirting the settlement and campground, to finish at the southwestern extremity of the bay.

A headland of sufficient size to carry its own name on coastal maps, arched out in a crescent to the right, its smooth grassy flanks falling gently to the black boulders of the beach. Halfway out stood a pandanus palm, rather the worse for wind, and it was beneath this that I sat . . . transfixed.

From the eastern tip of the point there rolled down into the bay, line after line of perfectly formed waves that peeled along the shoreline with absolute consistency. It wasn't their size that impressed, for at most they might only have been four foot. It was the simple flawlessness of their shape, the symmetry and physics of their peel.

In the fading light of that evening I knew that everything I had ever read of 'the North Coast' had its credence in the scene before me. Somehow the clichés fell into place. And just as certainly I knew that what I had for that short time was something delicate. A fragile thing that was best left undisturbed for the last minutes of useable light. I would not surf that evening. I would not hassle with the crowd off the point. That would come tomorrow if the swell held.

For the moment it was enough to sit and watch and know that as far as I was concerned the word had taken form.

I asked myself, whether it was T.S. Eliot's Magi who'd had a hard time of their journey, and chose to travel at night, questioning whether it was a folly.

I wasn't exactly sure, but gazing out from beneath the pandanus that evening, I knew that all of this was *my* sea folly.

ONE MAN'S MEAT

Sometime around mid-afternoon we drew level with the lighthouse and a fair old sea was running. Thirty-five year old timber cutters can have a tendency to leak, and for us time was now being measured in terms of pumping sessions. At that stage it was once every hour and a half, otherwise the water came up above the galley floorboards.

If nothing else the sea is always neutral. It gives and takes with total impartiality, which is something we romantics find difficulty in accepting. We are forever endowing it with spiritual qualities dragged from the depths of our own yearnings. We speak of it in the feminine gender, for neutrality and relentlessness, which are two of the sea's true characteristics, defy our fragile logic.

It was give-and-take that afternoon as we battled our way into a rising southerly and a steepening sea. A short distance to the west, behind the folds of Cape Byron, 'The Pass' would have been laying its long long lines down into the bay.

Somewhere abeam of the lighthouse the jib blew out along a seam line, and as I stood on the bowsprit attempting to restitch it, I remember that the bow was dipping into every second swell just enough to fill the rubber sea boots I was wearing and I wished the helmsman would ease us over them a little more gently. They were the same swells that would shortly be ridden at 'The Pass'.

As evening came on, our position, for the radio schedule with Sydney, was 'ten miles east of Ballina', and we were wet and tired.

Inside Byron they would have been surfed out. One man's meat is another man's poison.

FIREBRAND

For want of something better, at this stage let's just call him 'Firebrand'. He told me his home break was 'the North Coast . . .

all of it', and I had no reason to doubt him. He told me he'd surfed Burleigh and Kirra and Coffs and Crescent and Lennox and Byron and Snapper, and hundreds of other places besides, like Bells and Red Bluff and Cactus and Margarets and Boneyards and Infinities and Broulee, and all over the place without counting anything overseas. Indo, Hossegor, The Maldives, the North Shore, you name it.

He said that he surfed on a red board so that he'd stand out and that I'd be sure to know him when I saw him, but best keep out of his way, especially when he came off the lip or the bottom, because he was 'fast, mate, real fast'.

On the only day I saw Firebrand, he dinged some schoolkid's new board. Apparently the kid got in his way and shouldn't have been there at any rate.

Then he turned his attention onto me. Suggested that as I wasn't a local I'd best move on, the retirement village was up the beach. I said I'd stick around. Wanted to watch him. Firebrand smiled his sickly smile and slid onto the face of the afternoon's biggest left.

He cut a large S down its face and laid into his best bottom turn, the same one he'd seen on a million magazine pages. He faded, then gathered speed and came around for the climb back up the face.

Sensing a movement above his left shoulder Firebrand turned his head, just as the two-foot-thick lip took him straight in the neck and ground him down.

LIQUID DUES

In one sense at least surfing is no different from a lot of other things . . . progress demands a price. Improvement and competence, and ultimately perfection, exact their tolls, be they in time, money, pride or bruises. Or all four.

It had been described to me as 'a full-on left', and it was no understatement. In fact, at my level, on which there are no heroes or surf stars, it was just makeable, and with the bigger sets it shifted to my outer limits, the fifty-fifty region.

My first session out had its moments, but it was essentially safe, conservative and something I justified as getting the feel. There was never even an intimation of having it wired. Even so, I sensed that eventually I'd try to stay with it, at least part of the way, if only for the hell of it.

They were extremely hollow and heavy, of a type that has always given me trouble. Once you took the drop, and I mean 'the drop', there was no way out. No exit at all. You were committed for every last hair on your head, with rocks grinning at you only feet away, inches deep, and festooned with shellfish and sea urchins.

Around mid-morning I worked up to take on some of the bigger sets. It was the day's first mistake. Even as the horrifying descent began I sensed rather than saw a figure inside me. Effectively, I'd dropped in!

We hit the bottom together and wheeled in unison. There was no pulling off. It was a ride to the end and pray that I didn't come off in front of him, or hold him back, whoever he was.

Nothing happened, we made it through, he gave me an earful and I apologised. But it had the effect of unnerving me enough to decide to rest up out the back. And this *was* the day's fatal mistake.

Paddling seawards from the pack I allowed myself the luxury of rest, a break from the almost continuous struggle to position and justify my presence in the line-up. A startled hoot and the vision before me of the pack scratching its way towards me brought me out of it with a terrible dawning. To sea, but rapidly closing on us, were the week's two biggest waves. My advanced position had now become the takeoff point, and I was the only one on it.

Philosophers for centuries have argued the essence of freedom and the totality of choice. I possessed both, and yet sat totally condemned. Either I took the drop, and I already knew with a terrible flash of clairvoyance what that meant, or I passed it up to live forever with the derisive jeers of the pack ringing in my ears, and God knows there was already enough of that. Wheeling around I went for it.

The initial plunge was a free fall. Halfway down I realised that somehow the board was cocked all wrong and that if I didn't get the nose to lift I'd eat it at the bottom. It was a move from which I never recovered. The delicate balance came unstuck. I made the bottom but that was all. As it threw over my head, my last visual sensation was of silver and white descending about me.

Somehow I expected the worst in the intuitive way that takes over in those situations. Strangely, it didn't come, at least not right then. I think the whole impact was lessened by my having been inside and under the lip. Whatever the reason, it shook me up and bounced me around, sure, but it wasn't the worst I've had, not by a long shot. What it did do however was carry me to the edge of the rocks. And it was from here that the second wave of the set took over.

This time there was never a possibility of anything other than a thorough pasting. Euphemisms are strange things. Dusting, shakeout, shellacking, powdering. This one combined elements of them all. Initially it thumped, and then in quick succession rolled, pummelled, threw, shook, pounded, scratched and tore, before its merciful release. And all this in knee-deep water over the shellfish ledge.

I had a vague sensation of damage to my feet, which had borne the bulk of the initial impact. But it was only later, when I had extricated myself off the ledge amid the surgings of the smaller waves, that I saw the blood. My blood. The soles and tops of both feet had been thinly sliced, punctuated between with the black dots of sea urchin spines, each one of them deep enough to require extraction that night with a sterilised sewing needle.

Progress? Ah yes. Price? Toll? Dues? Fees? All paid . . . in full.

If it means anything at all, and I now know it doesn't, I might have wiped out, but I didn't pass it up. Surfers can rarely be saved, even from themselves.

NIGHT PASSAGE

The rolling had awakened me about midnight and for a time I lay listening to the rattle of the saucepans in the cupboard at the head of my bunk, and the hard metallic crack of the snubbing anchor chain as we came up short. The wind had not only got up while I slept, but had veered almost 180 degrees. It was now blowing more than 20 knots and what had been a sheltered anchorage at sunset was now a lee shore with a reef and beach just astern of us out there in the darkness.

A short while later I could take no more. Sleep had become impossible and I was already feeling vaguely ill. I got up, switched on the cabin light and retrieved the chart, pencils and dividers from the cabin floor. Bracing myself over a chart on the dinette table, I peered at the mass of detail spread out at my elbows. Shelter lay more than 50 kilometres to the north. What were a few hours of lost sleep, I reasoned, when the breeze was there for the taking?

I dressed, then heated a canned stew and made a cup of coffee. A moment later the motor was on and I stood at the foredeck fighting for each handhold of chain as the bowsprit tossed to the endless procession of swells that swept up from the southeastern horizon. With the anchor catted home over its roller, the bow fell off the wind to just a fraction west of north.

Easing the gearshift to neutral I ran forward to hoist the jib, crouching low to compensate for the rolling, hands shuttling from one hold to the next. The jib shot to the masthead, where it flapped and cracked like some demented beast, all alabaster in the moonlight. I sheeted it home and cut the motor. The yacht hissed along at four knots, its mast rolling wickedly against the sky.

For the next hour I sat huddled at the tiller, wrapped in a sleeping bag. The motion was uncomfortable and I felt the flushes of heat that precede seasickness. I stationed a bucket between my knees and tried to concentrate on the black outlines of land eight miles to port. But it didn't work and I knew that I had to steady the motion or succumb to seasickness.

Releasing the tiller I allowed the yacht to round up. As she did so, I threw off the sail ties and struggled with the heavy rolls of the mainsail. A moment of cursing, a heave on the halyard, and the sail billowed above me, the timber mast pulsing with its flogging.

I scampered for the cockpit and lifted the tiller to bring the wind just aft of the beam. Immediately the motion changed from the leisurely jaunt that the jib alone had given, to a breakneck charge with wind and sea. I trimmed the sheets and shone a torch at the speedo. We were doing a steady seven knots, with surges above that, and over the next hours it rarely fell as we ran off into the blackness of the night.

Every so often you make a passage that for some reason stands in the mind. Perhaps it was the fact that I was alone, or possibly the sheer sensation of speed, or more likely a combination of the two. But even as I sat there that night I knew I was in the middle of something special. I was alone, slightly apprehensive, vaguely seasick, and yet totally exhilarated.

At times the boat settled into a trough and all about her, dappled in silver, the seas boiled and bubbled like black oil. At other times she lifted, then somehow defying her ten tonnes and her four metre beam, shot forward with a long creaming stream of foam shooshing from the bows.

I sat in the cockpit until almost 5 a.m. when a terrible tiredness came over me. The moon had set and I could discern no trace of the coming day. Ahead I tried to pick up the flash of the lighthouse, but it was not to be seen.

I crawled over the aft decking and leaned out to engage the self-steering. Then for a time I sat on the pushpit railing, gripping the backstay. The wind vane of the self-steering was not entirely effective and every so often a wave would slew the stern across, causing an overcorrection to occur. But the average of both was a satisfactory course and I decided there was nothing better I could do than sleep. I crawled below to my bunk, acutely conscious of the noises of the water racing past the hull just centimetres from my ears.

I slept for an hour. It was close to 6 a.m. when I awoke and saw with relief the grey dawn sky through the open hatchway. I got up and looked out through the forward porthole. There in the greyness, amid the vivid whiteness of the tumbling seas, blinked the lighthouse and below it the sheltering folds of the cape.

A short time later I anchored and breakfasted on three fried eggs and a piece of toast. How good it was to be alive.

Coming up to Speed

From the very beginning it's one of those feelings that hovers with you like cigarette smoke at the edge of your vision. It's there but it defies definition or any attempt to pin it down, forever receding from the grasp like the bird of paradise. It will probably stay with you like that for the rest of your life and you'll return to seek it out time and time again.

A coastal road and a long unending seaway can make their way to a million destinations of the mind and spirit. When you live in the 'far south' as I do, it follows that almost everything else is 'the north' and in the beginning you're only ever as good as the word that gets back to you. As almost any Victorian surfer can tell you, water temperature, distance and the weight of the waves are the perennials that create our mindsets.

Every one of us starts the journey from a different place, and first impressions have always been important. Somehow the incredible mess inside us, the illusions and dreams, the spun gold of hearsay and rumour and drunken stoned snatches of conversation from somewhere down memory lane, needs concrete evidence that years of magazines, films and DVDs, 'oohs' and 'aahs', and the word of mouth, all have some basis of fact.

In the very beginning a notion has been taken, massaged, filtered, given a spin perhaps, and tossed our way. But it's then up to us to make of it what we will and no amount of plastic surf product can ever take that right away, nor the responsibility to ourselves that goes with it. We may start out as winter-frozen optimists, but eventually we're cast into the melting pot of something far bigger and infinitely more important — the stoke that has welded surfers together since time immemorial, wherever land presents itself to the ocean.

That first tank of fuel or perhaps the dropping of a mooring line begins a momentum that will always carry you through, because whatever lies you've heard about the coast and its healing sea, they're all true if you choose to make them so!

The Day that Charlie Wilson Died

At 6 a.m. that morning, as Robert Sloan awoke tight-faced and heavy-lidded, Charlie Wilson's boat was lifting to the gentle swells half a kilometre southeast of Raymond Head.

It was a good morning to be awake and Charlie breathed in deeply. Close by inshore, just off the rocky headland, he could see the heads of surfers, bobbing together like clusters of seals, rising and falling. One of them waved to him. It was Ray Hendy's new deckhand, a kid they called 'Swampy'. Charlie Wilson waved back.

Robert Sloan breathed in deeply too, but he felt slightly stale as he stretched his ample frame to its height and wrestled his body into the well-rehearsed routine of yet another day at the office.

It had not been a good season for Charlie Wilson. The crayfish catches had been slow, he'd lost pots in the gales earlier in the year, the fisheries people were talking of yet further tightening of the licence arrangements and the old Lister diesel in the *Ellen B* was giving problems. But as Charlie Wilson reasoned that dew-fresh morning in the swells southeast of Raymond Head, things could only look up. He'd been in fishing too long now to let a few slow weeks put him down, and besides, everything went in cycles. As the first of the yellow buoys marking his craypots came into view atop a swell, Charlie accepted that everything went in cycles — the weather, the swells, marriages, health, and fishing too.

The *Ellen B* was a heavy boat and as Charlie edged the tiller down with his thighs, she slowly came up to the wind 20 metres short of the first yellow buoy. Watching it as he did so, Charlie dropped the revs of the Lister diesel, threw the gear shift out with his foot, and let the *Ellen B* pitch to a standstill with the buoy on the starboard side.

Reaching over with a boathook, Charlie caught the line and drew it in, clasping hold of the wet plastic dome with its black-lettered initials 'CW'. Allowing the buoy to fall to the floor he took the rope leading from it, put two turns around the winch, threw the clutch, and casually paid the retrieved line onto the boards at his feet.

At first it appeared as a dull grey shape, but as it neared the surface the cane strands of the craypot took definition. In behind them could be seen the blurred, reddish-brown shapes of the crayfish. As the first strands of the pot broke the surface and dragged up the side of the hull, Charlie threw the clutch, then lifted the pot into the boat onto the floor in front of him. As he did so, he could hear the crayfish grinding and flapping. He reached in and one by one removed the three of them, checked them for size and sex, then placed two into the well in the centre of the *Ellen B* and returned one to the water.

It was a good enough start and Charlie was pleased as he placed the pot on the foredeck. Later, he would rebait it and reset it, perhaps at Desolation Rocks, where the big swells broke on the outer reef. But first he would retrieve his other pots.

As these things were happening, in the swells off Raymond Head that morning, Robert Sloan stood before his bathroom mirror. A towel was wrapped around his waist and traces of white shaving cream hung to his face like imitation snowflakes on a Christmas tree. He looked at himself and smiled. He had a friendly face and an optimistic manner went with it. He liked people and they generally liked him.

Another good day, he thought to himself, but God look at that waistline! How does that happen, he mused. Creeps up on you bit by bit, when you're too busy to notice. He wiped away the last traces of the shaving cream and dabbed aftershave on his cheeks and jowls. Maybe I should start a gym program, he thought to himself. As he closed the bathroom door another thought came forward. Maybe I could stay with Greg Mayne at his holiday place down on the coast, and he could get me back into surfing. It was good when we did it and maybe I could get a big board and try again. Maybe.

When Robert Sloan reached the kitchen a short time later, his wife was about to leave for work.

'So what happens today?' she asked, downing the last of her coffee.

'Not a great deal, except that at 9.30 a.m. Jim Davidson comes in and signs the contract on those houses down by the bay,' Robert Sloan replied. 'Funny, isn't it? I worked hard on three others to take them as one lot and he just came in out of the blue. He's going to pull them all down and do what he calls "an integrated, maritime-themed development".'

'Well, what say we go out and celebrate?' his wife asked.

'What a good idea,' Robert Sloan said. 'Yes, let's go out and celebrate. I'll have a drink at the office first and meet you at 6.30 p.m. at The Orange Tree. How's that sound?'

Like so many other things in life it was easily settled and Robert Sloan went on alone to finish his breakfast. It would not be an exceptional day and by noon, to all intents and purposes, the important work part of it would be over. But that was the way he liked it, quick and clean, not too much prevaricating, and with something in it for everybody.

By now the sun was shining. Charlie Wilson felt it warming him through the heavy knit of his grey sweater. The catch hadn't been great. It lay in the well at his feet. Seven crays and a couple of parrotfish. Overhead a mollyhawk and a group of gulls wheeled and squawked. Charlie reached over and took the smallest of the parrotfish. It was now dead and the brightness of its body was fading to a dull scaly white stiffness.

Cutting it into small pieces, Charlie flung them to the birds a piece at a time. At first it was the larger bird that took each bit.

But then Charlie began to throw to the smaller gulls, and as if sensing the favouritism being shown them, they moved in closer to the boat and took them before they hit the water. Charlie was pleased. There was something for everybody.

A light northerly was blowing as Charlie took the *Ellen B* around the coast to Desolation Rocks. Occasionally a breaking wave top would burst against the bow, throwing a shower of soft foam down the boat. Charlie had braced himself in the after-steering well, feet astride, the tiller pressed between his buttocks. It freed his hands to work the bait, and as the *Ellen B* cut through the swells Charlie reached down and took the hessian bag with the meat and fish heads and placed it in front of him.

Throttling back he disengaged the gear lever and allowed the boat to slow until all forward movement ceased, and it pitched and rolled silently on the swells. Charlie took the baits and tied them inside each of the craypots on his foredeck. When that was done he arranged them in pairs and checked that their lines and buoys were ready to run free without tangling.

Now he was ready for Desolation Rocks. There could be only one run at it, straight down the line, and if the pots weren't placed properly that was too bad. It was only difficult if you didn't know how, but Charlie Wilson knew how. When Hendy and all the others stuck close to the reefs around Raymond Head, Charlie Wilson worked the corridor between the cliff and Desolation Rocks. It was all a matter of timing and Charlie knew he had it. Deep down inside it was one thing he knew he had and didn't need to talk about.

Robert Sloan sat in his office as the hour approached. He was full of coffee, amped up and nervous. It was usually this way when the actual moment approached. It wasn't an unpleasant feeling; in fact he liked the intensity it added to things. In the beginning almost every sale was like this, but now it was only the big ones. All the others, the houses, apartments, small shops and suburban blocks he could do easily. But the city and shopping mall developments, the coastal estate projects and country clubs still had that edge to them, and he hoped it would always be that way. After all this time he could do it well. He knew that, and others did too. Sure, there was stress in it, but it was all worthwhile when the thing was done.

The contracts lay before him on the desk. Robert Sloan wondered how many times he had waited like this. A blank space at the bottom of a page, with space for a signature. It all seemed simple enough. Robert Sloan looked at his watch. It was just after 9.30 a.m. Jim Davidson would arrive at any minute.

As the *Ellen B* lifted on each swell Charlie could clearly see the rocks at the cliff base. Some 20 metres out from them, and running along parallel to them for perhaps 60 or 70 metres, was the dark line of the outer reef. It was down this corridor that he would take the *Ellen B* and set his pots.

Entering the eastern end of the gap, Charlie reduced speed and watched the greeny-black rocks of the reef slide past as he swung the boat to port. Locking the tiller with a wire peg to hold course, he leaned forward and reached for the first of the craypots. He lifted it alongside the boat, placed it in the water, then leaned over the side to make sure its line was not tangled. As the pot began to sink, Charlie let its line run free and then threw out its yellow buoy.

The *Ellen B* was steering herself down alongside the cliff face to starboard, rolling one way from the swell that came in, but tossing also to the backwash from the cliff. Charlie checked the course, picked up the second pot and bent to place it alongside in the water.

It was just as he did this that it happened.

As he leaned over, some configuration of swell and backwash came together, causing the *Ellen B* to lurch and roll heavily to starboard. Charlie's body was angled out from the cockpit and the movement caused his footing to slip. As the boat rolled across, he fell face first overboard, onto the cane and wire strands of the craypot.

His first sensation was of water pressing around him, then of its coldness as it seeped through his sweater and filled the yellow waterproof waders he was wearing. He looked up to see the boat still moving forward.

In one hand he held the line from the pot, and could feel the weight of the basket settling below him. If the other end held, and the plastic buoy somehow fouled on the boat then there was a chance he could drag himself back on board, or at least alongside. He clutched onto the line and watched as it ran out from the boat. For a moment it held as the yellow buoy came up from the floor and caught in the cockpit coaming. Charlie felt it begin to drag him through the water. Then, just as suddenly, it broke free and he saw it flip up and over the side. He was alone in the water now, and there was no longer any point in holding on to the line. He let it slip from his hand, and watched the *Ellen B* motor off away from him. He supposed she would be rolled on to the cliffs a few hundred metres down the shoreline.

His clothing was becoming waterlogged. He couldn't land on the rocks, the cliffs were too sheer and the swell too heavy. All he could think of to do was to try and swim for the beach a kilometre or more to the west. But his clothes were too heavy. Kicking to tread water he fumbled with the knotted cord holding his waders around his waist and into which his sweater had been tucked. The cord would not undo. His fingers couldn't feel the knot. He kicked his legs, but the weight pulling him down forced him to use his hands to keep his head above the water.

Now he was tired. It was becoming harder to rise to the waves and the tops were sometimes breaking over him. At first he held his breath, but then he began to pant and the air felt heavy and leaden. The waves began to wash across him as he panted, until one broke over him as he breathed in. He coughed and struggled, kicking with his legs, but the weight of the water-filled waders held his legs down. He splashed with his arms. His breathing sounded as if in an echo chamber.

A whiteness had now come before his eyes and suddenly he felt weak and relieved. It was easy now. It was easy to stop and let the warmth at the back of his head move forward. It was all so easy. He stopped kicking and allowed the whiteness to rise up and softly envelop him.

The contracts had been signed. Robert Sloan's work day was effectively done. He would bide his time in the office, have a long lunch and try to hold on to the warm feeling the sale had left. Later he would share it with his wife and try to hold it for as long as he could. It might last some days, but eventually it would fade and become something that he had done in the past and would be called on to do again. Tomorrow or the day after it would have to be done again. But today was the day of the sale, it was his day, and no one could deny that.

It was also the day that Charlie Wilson died.

Fat City

Even now, after all this time, I find it hard to write about Jacky Paradise and those last final days down on the coast. Some things I can remember as if they happened yesterday. But others are only a stirring, a shiver if you like, a remembrance caught up in the debris of my mind.

Where these things ever start I don't know. At the time he was up north somewhere, maybe it was Mareeba or Moree. Who knows? He was flat broke and I sent up a few dollars for the fare down. There was a scabies outbreak in the Aboriginal section of town and the southern press was having a field day with it. Even without that I never thought it would all happen the way it did. One of my old girlfriends used to talk about destiny, and perhaps that's what this really was, a dark wind that was always going to come in one day.

Jacky was quite amazing really. He was like a spirit that lived off the land. It was as if he never needed food or drink as you and I do, but drew his nourishment from everything that was about him wherever he was. One moment it was dust and the long ever-shimmering road, railway camps, empty wine flagons, fights and the shrill screams of frightened women. Then it was something else.

I don't think it mattered to him where he was. All places were the same. Two days after my call he was at the station. Just like that. How he did it I'll never know.

I'd waited for him on a seat down by the ticket box at the end of the platform. For a time I thought he hadn't made it. A lot of people had walked past me and I was near ready to give it away when up by the pedestrian footbridge that arches the tracks with its soot-stained wrought iron I saw him. A small black man with a pencil thin moustache and a grey felt hat, carrying a suitcase and a hessian sack of snakes.

I knew then I hadn't made a mistake. He was my man. The pros might arrive in town in their hire cars, boards, baggage, logos and all that paraphernalia stacked above them. But not Jacky. He had some dignity and style. Jacky was never plastic.

I have to admit that at that time I hadn't been to a single surfing contest in a long, long time. My feelings were more like those of a Merle Haggard song. It was like looking at life through a frosted windowpane, a type of trouble in mind. I sort of had this hope that Jacky would wipe the window clean and things would be clear again, like they used to be.

Fifteen years before this I'd been with him up north, boxing in his gym down by the old Manhattan Hotel. But I never thought things would work out the way they did. Even up to the moment he stepped off the rattler that autumn morning, I still believed there was a place for change in surfing. I never realised how far out of the mainstream I'd drifted.

On the Wednesday night before the surf contest I'd re-run that scratchy old '50s film of him in his first main event. He was only nineteen, and God he was good. Left hand, right hand, coming or going he could put you down just like that. Jab, hook, bob, weave, Jacky had all the moves. For a while there, a bit later, they started putting him in with some classy overseas imports and he still looked good.

When you're a black man and you've boxed there aren't too many people you trust. They say it's best to travel light, and that's the way he always did it. That's how he arrived in town the day they started the surf contest. A small black man with a suitcase, a sack of snakes and a felt hat.

He told me once that early in his career he'd railed down south for a preliminary fight, and they'd tried to set him up. 'Those big stations are lonely places on a Monday morning,' he said, 'city noise, white tiles, wine bottles and brown paper bags.' He'd stayed at an old YMCA, with its all-pervading stench of disinfectant, and the incessant coughing that came from behind almost every door.

They told him they'd arrange the corner for him. 'We'll save you a few quid, son,' they said, 'no need to bring anybody down with you. We'll put one of the best local trainers in your corner.' When three of the preliminaries fell short they rescheduled him for ten rounds as the main support. It took him just three of those rounds to realise his corner had their money on the other boy. It made no difference. When he won in the fourth they didn't like it. They told him he was finished. 'You won't be used down here again, mate,' they said, which proved to be incorrect.

Nothing had changed the morning I picked him up. All the booze and the shit jobs didn't matter, I knew he could still make the moves if he had to. His eyes were just as I'd always remembered them. Soft and dark and deep. Time and tent fights hadn't dimmed them one iota.

The same night that I had watched the film of Jacky's epic bout, a depression had deepened in the high latitudes of the Southern Ocean. Its early movements went uncharted, but its centre was later registered at 998 hectopascals. Sure, the winds near its centre were strong, but its main influence on my life was felt when it tightened up the pressure gradients on the preceding high.

Around the time I'd arrived at the station the synoptic chart showed long westerly lines laid out like furrows in a wheat field. They began the contest that same morning in surf the media described as 'historic'. At the time I wondered what they meant, but it became clear soon enough.

By the time Jacky and I reached the beach a big swell was rolling. Big? I would say ten foot with much bigger sets. At that stage they were coming in rows of three or four every six minutes, and some of the pros were having trouble getting out. In fact just as we stepped down onto the beach a figure had materialised on the sand beside us. It was one of the Americans.

He'd tried twice and hadn't been able to clear the rocks. He was tired, just back from the brink of drowning and strung out. By the time he'd walked down the beach to below the flags and the judging stands his anger had him.

Barely ten metres from us he dramatically flung his board onto the sand, and looking over our heads at the crowd on the clifftop above he screamed, 'You motherfuckers . . . you sons of bitches . . . whadda ya mean sending us out in that, you bastards!' I don't know if it was directed at the judges or the crowd, but it made no difference. A few people laughed and that was it.

Jacky and I passed up along the beach beside the windmill, to where the old creek had once flowed. On the southern side there was a coarse gravel mound, and above it a bent tea-tree cut the skyline. Jacky still had his suitcase and the sack with the snakes. He looked terribly out of place. I wasn't beside him when he started talking so I don't really know how it all began.

Actually I was staring out to sea to where an albatross, a fully mature Wanderer, was rising and falling in a long lonesome glide above the swells at the horizon's edge. They aren't a common sight so close to land just here, and when I turned to tell Jacky I realised he was a little distance off, standing on the incline of the gravel mound talking, and what's more that people were listening. Not only that, the group was quickly swelling as people pressed forward to hear what he was saying.

Style dictates some things, and it is probably better now if I don't even attempt to précis what he said. I guess the gist of it was what is described in the popular press as 'the notion of freedom', or 'liberation', or 'discovering one's way'. But those terms hardly do it justice. It centred strongly around individual responsibility, making up your own mind about things, and certainly wasn't anything even vaguely related to what church hierarchies, social agencies, business and other vested interests put forward. But I think that's how most people still see it, as a serpent to be ground under heel.

Sometime around the point Jacky first used the word 'salvation', or maybe it was 'freedom', I'm not quite sure, The Businessman drew me aside. He'd seen the crowd gathering and had come down to investigate. 'Salvation' wasn't a word he felt very comfortable about, even though Jacky's use of it had nothing at all to do with the whole notion of sin, as promulgated by the churches.

'Isn't this bullshit?' he said by way of an opening.

'Not at all,' I replied. 'You of all people should know that revival meetings don't happen down here.' I tried to personalise it by emphasising the 'you', hoping somehow he'd take it on board, even file it away and maybe get to it later. It was always so difficult trying to talk to him, to pin him down.

'There's a bit more to this than meets the eye,' I eventually added.

'I'll bet there is,' he said. 'Why the hell did you set this thing up? We're the only ones who know what's cool, and this isn't. What were you hoping to achieve?'

I looked at him. 'It isn't a set up. It was always going to happen,' I said. 'Being cool is like trying to dam up water.'

I heard him mutter 'Oh fuck!' under his breath and he looked away. Then he turned back and his voice was suddenly very strong and clear, but not loud. 'As far as we're concerned down here,' he said, 'the Government's tax package is bullshit. Companies with loads of debt or heavy overseas borrowings are likely to find their interest rates eating into profits. Sure, you can hedge but increased liquidity's the thing. Don't fall for the two-card trick of rising costs and falling sales, and above all don't be blinded by conventional wisdom.'

At that time I didn't actually know what he was talking about; I was still just a surfer, at least in my own mind. But there was worse to follow. He paused and his eyes ran out across the beach and along the line of the clifftop crowded with people. 'The economic reality is that the dollar is volatile,' he said. 'If I put so much as one foot wrong now I'm a dinosaur in the economic desert. All this gone. I can wave Wall Street goodbye.' His hands gestured in a general sweep, and then, 'Real interest rates are here to stay. Get yourself a good tax accountant and a condo in Tahiti. That's the reality of surfing these days, not this ... this ... "freedom bullshit".'

In retrospect I think the length of the statement exhausted him. He wasn't given to sharing his thoughts with too many people, and even at the time I knew that in some sense I was being given as good a piece of him as it was possible to get. Earlier that same morning I'd seen him watching the waves through a pair of binoculars. He'd told me then that his main concern in life now was not how to make the drop onto another waveface, but only to find sufficient space on his T-shirts for another logo. He started to babble about 'branding', or something, but it sounded like mutton dressed up as lamb to me. 'This cotton polyester is wonderful stuff,' he'd said, 'a man could get involved with it in a personal way.'

Strangely, just two months after all this he went into receivership. His creditors had pulled the pin. One of them was talking about sending in some heavies, and possible 'tissue damage'. Under the circumstances, calling in the receivers was probably the best option for everyone.

Late in my dialogue with him, at almost the same instant he spat out the term 'freedom bullshit', a gasp went up from the crowd around us. I knew what it meant. I'd heard it too many times before not to know, and in the early days I'd heard it slide from my own mouth. It meant Jacky had the snakes out.

I don't know if you've ever seen what happens to a crowd when the snakes come out. All those years of unfaced fears, forgotten childhood stories nurtured in the backblocks of the mind, the horror, the pale dry-mouthed clamminess and the nervous bravado — well, it all comes together. The crowd gets restless, it falls back from the front like a wheat field before the wind, and sways with an almost sexual movement. Screams, and laughter devoid of any real substance, wash back and forth in a surge of fear. That's how it happened that morning at the back of the beach.

The first place I'd ever seen it had been one time when Ram Chandra performed in Townsville. But that performance had been entertainment pure and simple. This was different. This came in from the desert like a summer storm, in from the aeons of time, from the genetic implanting at the dawn of man. It touched on the inner fear that lies in all of us, the one we always carry and contact sometimes in the early hours of the morning. Spooky and best left undisturbed.

I now found myself not knowing whether to look at Jacky, his arms festooned with snakes, writhing and alive, held up as if to shelter his face from the sun, or at the disbelieving group that stood around him.

The surfing had long ceased to matter. I no longer knew what was going on. There were ten-foot swells and they were sending out heat after heat. All I remember now is coloured singlets, jerky movements and a droning commentary that ran on and on in the background.

When I looked around to see how The Businessman was handling all this, I realised he'd gone, faded off into the background like a vapour. The people around me were total strangers and I looked everywhere for a familiar face. It was some time before I caught sight of The Kid. He'd changed of course, but sure as eggs it was him all right, sitting in a director's chair at the edge of the cliff.

I'd last seen him the same year he won all those contests and I'd never forgotten the speed he could generate on a waveface. For a while there he was unbeatable and the press acknowledged that he'd 'changed the direction of surfing'. It was a pretty big call but I had no real beef with it. I know the boards were different then, but he was never staccato, there was nothing mechanical or predictable in the way he surfed, and certainly none of that jumping up and down trying to carry through to the six-inch re-form on the beach. If the wave was finished, or wasn't there in the first place, neither was he. His surfing flowed, if that's the phrase. He always came off as smoothly as he stroked in.

No sponsors had ever got hold of him either, in any shape or form. He was too much of a maverick for them. He never had any money, and he only ever got out of Australia once. His type of outlook couldn't handle going foreign, and all the bullshit associated with leaving home. The only time he went he was back inside a month, but even today, after all this time, they still talk about him over there.

No logos, no corny beach fashions ever hung off him, and you never saw him in those contrived magazine ads either. But it killed him just the same. It has a habit of doing that. The longer you think you've kept your options open, the harder the gate finally snaps shut. We're all a bit fragile, I guess. And when the lights go out, if you can't see in the dark you've got problems.

I knew he'd battled alcohol — God knows I'd been with him enough in the early days to see what it was doing to him. After that it was heroin, and now it was cancer. Somehow he'd dragged himself down to the clifftop and sat there beside his wife, white-faced and pencil thin, just staring out. I don't know what thoughts were going through his mind. He was dead within six months. I found out later that on the morning he died he'd somehow crawled from his hospital bed to the window, and had collapsed from the effort of trying to raise the glass windowpane to breathe fresh air.

Jacky's talk finished fairly quickly. To be absolutely honest I don't think it had very much impact on most people. Sure, the snakes had impressed them for a time, but a steady diet of videos and DVDs seemed to have laid waste whatever fertile ground there might have been. A notion like 'freedom', even with snakes, can't ever hope to compete with DVDs, plastic product, and the rest of the noise out there. Once Jacky finished it was all downhill for us really.

Our first and only trouble came later, in the evening at the presentation. It was waiting for us when we arrived, thicker than the cocaine crystals on the toilet floor, and just as slippery as the food plastered all over the dance floor. 'I think we should give this one a miss,' I'd said, but Jacky was adamant we should stick it out to the end. He had some notion that to bail out early was never the best way to go. After a day on the beach he wanted a drink, especially after the snakes escaped in the backyard of my rented house, and my neighbours became agitated.

We began on a flagon of cheap port. Around us it was chaos. Somewhere in the lighted areas up front a presentation of sorts began. There were surfers wearing dinner suits, making speeches thanking their sponsors and each other. Prizes and cheques were being thrown about like so much confetti, but at the back of the hall where we were, no one knew or cared what was going on.

A constant stream of food rained from one side of the hall to the other, glasses and bottles were spilt and broken at almost every table. Figures lay slumped on the floor, or against the walls, two of them with pools of vomit beside them. Between tables, and on the dance floor, over-amped figures gyrated this way and that, pushing and groping. Scuffles broke out here and there with angry strident voices. A woman was punched when she accidentally backed into someone at the edge of the dance floor.

In the midst of this mess I spotted trouble for us fairly early in the proceedings. He was wearing some sort of singlet because I remember his bare shoulders and the tattoos, and the way he'd stood back and sized us up. He must have thought about it for a while, because for a time nothing happened, and then he just sort of lunged at us out of the darkness.

'When I think of all the work that's been done to get surfing on its feet,' he was shouting at us, 'all the self-sacrifice for our sport, the people who have given up absolutely everything to make it a mainstream sport, I could . . . I could . . . '

He paused, momentarily lost for the right words. As his voice trailed off I thought we were out of it. But no such luck. 'And now this turns up,' he went on, his eyes glancing at Jacky, 'this fucking freedom crap.'

Before I realised how pissed he was I thought we were going to have real trouble. But just two steps back from us he launched his punch like someone heaving a shot-put. It missed by a mile. His own momentum took him stumbling past Jacky, face first into the table edge and then to the floor. At least that's how I saw it.

There was another view that Jacky's hands had moved. Nobody was sure of anything except the guy's teeth were gone in a bubble of bloody foam and a muffled groan.

'Oh shit,' I heard someone say, and after that I'm not sure of anything, because it all just erupted. We got out the side door before the police arrived, but we'd been worked over. It wasn't just us, there were others too. At one stage I'd warded off a broken bottle with my arm. A deep jagged cut was sliced into the flesh below the elbow, and it bled profusely, thick and deep red, down over my hand and fingers.

As we rested up in the darkness of the car park Jacky pressed his hands over the cut, holding it together. For a time I saw a stain oozing out from between his stumpy, short-nailed fingers, and felt a heat where the pressure of his fingers was against my arm. When he took his hand away, loose blood was still on my arm but the cut had gone. I wiped the blood away and all that remained was a thin pink line, like a surgical scar. The cut itself had gone. Just like that. It had gone.

Jacky never said a thing, not then, nor at any stage later.

I knew then that something had changed forever. The tide had been full and now it had turned. The mud flats of middle age can distance you from a lot of things, but that night I suddenly realised it was all finished for me. What was it someone had once written about 'the courage to lose sight of the shore'? How far offshore does a surfer ever go? One hundred and fifty metres? Fifteen hundred metres?

I left Jacky at the station two days after all this. To this day I don't even know who won the contest. It's all the same after a while, and it's all been made to look the same.

Our faces were still puffy, red and blotched. Both my eyes were blackened, blue–yellow like the inside of hard-boiled eggs. Jacky's skin was sallow from the port. He hadn't stopped drinking since the snakes escaped. His hands were shaking.

That same morning he left we'd stood on a headland down from the rented house. The wind had laid down the coastal grasses and a moan had set up in the stunted trees. High above us, in the absolutely cloudless blue sky, six ibis had come down the coast, north to south. Things had been wet that autumn and lots of the nearby paddocks had low-lying water in them. Moments later another group of four appeared, then another. Soon they numbered perhaps fifteen or twenty birds.

At first the flight had no structure to it. It circled and wheeled, this way and that. But at last a central core of circling in only one direction began to establish itself, and it was to this group that the others attached themselves. In this way the circle became bigger and bigger, the birds no longer black spots but now a mass, cohesive and purposeful. They then streamed out into a gigantic V that turned inland against the wind, and away from the sea.

I took this to mean the swell would drop out, which it did.

It was hinted to me later by my therapist that these things never really occurred. But I know they did. Some things are true even if they never happened. I know Jacky's now up north. When I last spoke to him he was running a prawn trawler somewhere up on the Queensland coast. He won't come down again in a hurry. He told me it's too cold south of Brisbane.

There's also the thin surgical-like scar on my left forearm. If all of this never happened, then how did that get there, and what healed it?

Earth Journey

THE GUIDING LIGHTS

'Nothing is, but what is not,' Handley had told me, almost Macbeth-like, one surfed-out Saturday evening. In the darkness outside, beyond the house, the Otway fogbanks were falling fast about us like heavy blankets of biblical retribution. Kitchen-sitting in the benevolent glow of the crackling logs I heard him add his afterthought: 'It's your own affair. The bird of paradise lands only on the hand that doesn't grasp.' And then he laughed.

So that was it, was it . . . the bird of paradise?

Handley's visions of surfing had always been a little nebulous. In fact I don't think he'd ever quite got over having that empty beer bottle thrown at him from a passing car on his first night in Sydney after six months in Tennant Creek. He'd come back down to surf, and while he could comfortably handle the pub brawls up north, the ceaseless undercurrent of the city always disturbed him. There was also the theft of his ten-foot-six Vic Tantau Tear Drop from the tea-tree at Waratah Bay in the early 1960s. It had somehow disturbed his concept of order in the universe that someone could ever *find* the board, let alone steal it.

And now, years later, a farewell of sorts tucked up on a ridgeline above Apollo Bay. Handley was headed to the US, and I was making for the North Coast on yet another highway that hopefully had a wave at the end of it . . . and maybe even along it.

'When you reach California,' I said to him jokingly, 'you must get yourself an analyst, and maybe slide into one of those therapeutic institutes and we'll arrange for Bobby Zimmerman and Joan Baez to visit you.'

'And Robert Altman,' Handley said. 'Bianca Jagger and Jacques Cousteau.'

Then the lunacy of the visitors' list swept over us, just as quickly as the tide of American culture that underpinned it. Names were pressed forward for inclusion, a lot of them popular press darlings of the day, some Australian but most American. They included the Reverend Jesse Jackson, Elmer Gantry, Tammy and Jim Bakker, the Bronzed Aussies, David Nuuhiwa, and twenty-five or thirty others.

We laughed, but two of the Australian names had touched something real for me: Dan Morgan, the bushranger they'd labelled 'Mad Dog', and Les Darcy, the doomed Australian middleweight boxer. Fighting men who'd stood against the wind. A surf trip could be most things, and where I was heading almost anything could be conjured up from nothing. But it all needed a peg, a something to hang it on. It needed to make sense, not just to the emotions but to the mind as well.

If Handley were right, and I had no doubt he probably was, then a lot of what was about to unfold would be of my own making, and if that were the case then two lonely graves, Morgan's at Wangaratta and Darcy's at East Maitland, might just mean something in the translucent wastes of a surfing life. A pile of earth and a granite headstone. I marked them in as stops along the way, knowing I needed a cerebral balance to the unceasing demands of the surf.

'It's up there all right, but you've got to find it for yourself,' someone had said to me. Handley told me, 'It's your own affair,' and that's how I'd always seen it, but with that extra dimension of sinking my feet into the Australian earth.

Ten days later in the pre-dawn hours of a drizzle-grey Victorian autumn morn the road took over. In the 5.15 a.m. chill I took the freeway out, senses ablaze, eyes agleam, to join and pick up and fuse with the traffic trickles and tributaries and streams and raging rivers of a city-Wednesday work machine, sucking in the fodder of another day.

I sat encapsuled in my own visions, and swept along past joggers tripping the grey fantastic, their feet pitter pattering the roadways and paths, past grim stony-faced workers and headscarfed women who stood at tram stops and stared at the crazed apparition before them, beanie pulled over his ears and surfboards stacked up from the roof above.

Was it only yesterday that I had stroked alone and unseen onto that six-foot morning swell down south? A short walling left, out from a bank below a clifftop saltbush, with split second images of something 'up there', its lip wobbling, edged in white, and a sense that if I came forward on the board I might yet make it through. And now, just twenty-four hours later, north city blacks and greys glimpsed from between the grating slide-slide of windscreen wipers, as the rain-splattered streams thickened and swept me along in their inevitable preordained paths to the factories and offices of the city fringe.

And then at just one last set of traffic lights, with the traces of dawn licking the eastern sky, the mass of cars about me turned left for the Ford plant and a day's labour, and I slid free and alone on to the first reaches of the highway out, flashing to the realisation that this was it.

The thing had been done and now it quickly gathered its own momentum, rolling through successive days in a never-stop-not-even-for-petrol blast to the end. Time flashed past, lost in a nimbus of pulsating billboard signs that read such things as Tropic Waters Motel, El Greco Nirvana Lodge, Fresh Prawns Now — all floating by loosely in the day's light.

Place names appeared and reappeared. Road signs came up then rolled past, totally without meaning, so that swinging into another bend at 95 ks the mind would recall some other sign (was it that one I've just passed?) and wonder had it read 35 ks or 85 ks. Moments of strange tranquillity too, beside autumn-willowed creek beds, and country cemeteries. Morgan's grave a dismal pile; Darcy's a pot of gold at 7 a.m. with the solitary whistling moan of a passing freight train in the East Maitland gloom.

'Nothing is but what is not,' Handley had said to me.

POSSUMS

When the earth journey first unfolded for me, I surfed a spot they called 'Possums', down beside an old river mouth. It was midweek. The drive had taken its toll, and I arrived almost sleepless. I was too amped up. It was being called the biggest swell of the year, but I'd chosen somewhere away from the full brunt of it. In the car park I heard somebody say how hopeless it was with drop-ins on ten-foot waves.

I had the good fortune to make it out almost without even getting my hair wet. Seven were in the line-up, but only two were genuine starters; the others shell-shocked and under gunned. There is just one wave from that day I remember, because I couldn't get off it, and I wanted to. As fast as I worked my way down the line, it came with me, walling and feathering just 'there' at my shoulder. Twice it threw out over me. It took me from the outside reef to damn near the inside beach, and at the finish I got off only by pulling down the front as it walled up to collapse, and then proning out. The vision I had as it did so was of being caught in an energy release in which I didn't really belong.

In the car park afterwards two guys drove by and told me how they felt about tourists coming to their break. They didn't actually stop their car. The abuse all came as they snaked past me in the red gravel. There was also some mention of what they would do to me the next time they found me there. I just laughed. There probably wouldn't be a next time, I thought to myself. Welcome to the road.

COUNTRY DREAM 1

It might have been the central East African coast somewhere north of Mombassa, for the beach was barren and the guide was a strange old Arab called 'The Captain of the World'.

But instinctively and without explanation we knew it was Australia. It might have been the Bight or somewhere with yellow sandstone headlands and sparse desert-type vegetation. To sea there was breaking an absolutely monumental grinding left-hander, that peaked up, its top feathering droplets in the dry offshore breeze, then peeled, staccato fashion — click, click, click — like the frozen frames of a film. And all this under a cloudless sky and a dry white light.

The Captain of the World was going to take us out there in his canoe, and he would stand on the beach in his strange striped gown and skull cap with his gnarled and whiskered face, and point his left arm out at the break. As he did so we would find ourselves looking down into the depths of that peeling chasm.

We loaded our gear into the canoe and The Captain of the World poled us out with the long sweeps of his oars that were rowlocked near the stern of the canoe.

In the first ages there had been no one else, and The Captain of the World had seen the headlands and beaches of the coast totally without company. His had been the legend that had laid out the way for others who widened and bitumenised then developed and sub-divided the lot as beach estates. But in his time he had thought nothing of it, and his innocence had precluded any realisation of what it was that might happen. To him it had been sustained by its own momentum. It had rolled and flowed and flooded the corners of his life like an ether that eventually took him from the heavy cold greens of the south to the rich thick humid warmth of the north. And now he was by the desert with its crumbling cliffs and desperate vegetation.

At one time he had lain over the coastal belt like a vapour, visiting the landlocked farmers of the west to talk of the mysteries of the ocean, or sitting out lonely six-week vigils with the fishermen on the beach waiting for the mullet schools that were passing in the night and could not be netted, and camping on the headlands of the seaboard with the sounds of the surf ringing clear in the crystal stillness of the midwinter nights. With fires crackling, dancing and throwing their flames of warmth, he would sit and let those other waves wash up from within.

It seemed very important to me that The Captain of the World knew clearly and with complete exactness everything I was thinking. As the dream faded I was looking deeply into his black, black eyes and trying to get him to realise what I was thinking and why.

I still don't know whether he understood, for he had begun to turn the canoe around and paddle back to shore.

FLIGHT

It was an east coast headland, ever soft in the morning light, its waters sparkling under the day's first rays and throwing totally translucent shapes of pale green and silver, back lit and ethereal.

The takeoff point was perhaps 400 metres from the camp, out along the sand flats with their moulded wave patterns swirling in untrodden innocence. A bevy of gannets and gulls hovered above, ever anxious for the pickings of the pilchard schools.

First light, and four out. But that would change quickly. Utopia could be a parlous thing, and in the final estimation its existence hung in the balance of human attitude. Changes would occur later that morning, of that I was sure. Changes. That's just what the incoming camp supervisor had told me earlier were going to take place all round.

'Hey, you,' he had called out to me the morning before, 'what time do they open the store around here?'

'It's supposed to open at 8 a.m.,' I replied. 'I'm waiting like you.'

'Yeah?' he said. 'Well from next week on there's gonna be a few changes made.'

'How's that?' I asked.

'I'm takin' over,' he said.

I wasn't sure what I was meant to say and just blurted out, 'Oh, some changes.'

'Yeah. For a starter the store'll open at 6.30 a.m., and there'll be breakfast available for fellas like you,' he said.

Fellas like me. That was something.

Well things would change all right, of that I was certain. By mid-morning eighteen would be in the line-up, and an hour later twenty-five, at which stage the barely useable beachbreak down from the headland would start to offer its uncomplicated compensations. There could be no solitary surfing 400 metres from a crowded camp ground. That was a thing for other places in some other age, and I knew the realities as well as anybody else. Handley had spelt them out that night at Apollo Bay. And I also knew that the whole had many parts, that the number out would alter but a lot of other things would not.

Not the cloudless sky with its subtle sweep of blues, not the green grassy slopes of the headland with its backdrop of mountains standing in relief on the horizon like the spinal undulations of some primitive creature. Not even the flawlessness of those morning shapes with their hollow sections that glinted from deep inside as if sheltering some unknown, ever-beckoning promise of silvery silence and rest. Not the first cooling washes of that lean clean sea about the feet, nor the foam that fell about you as you pushed out alive with that particular expectancy only a surfer knows when the waves are there.

Not any of these things would change.

Six out was one thing, but twenty-five was another. For a short time it had actually held together as waves cleared the take-off with a mechanical regularity, and the six of us could rotate and ride with never a thought as to just how far inside you might have to be to even have an inkling of a theoretical 'right of possession' for the next takeoff. That was something that came later as the numbers grew and the subtle hues changed, and the uncomplicated social structure broke down under the assaults of number, and the reality that accompanied the fact that if you made no effort at all, then you simply got no waves, and that was not what you were there for. It's the same process that repeats itself every single day at every single half-decent surf break on any day with waves.

The early morning entity with its innocence and cohesion was lost somewhere around the arrival of the tenth surfer, and buried for the day with the fifteenth. From a distance I had for some reason half assumed he was acting for the benefit of his mates. The frantic half-crazed strokes, the perpetual motion, and the constant side glances to check that no one got inside him, seemed a satire of surfing's worst excesses. It was not until I got up close enough to hear the broken phrases muttered to himself, and the eyes that bounced from one side to the other, that I knew it was no act. There was probably some chemical additive to it all.

'No one's takin' this . . . they'd fuckin' do it . . .' The words flowed from him like water from a leaking main. It was only as the next set loomed up that I realised with a terrible dawning the cause of his agitation. It was simply the possibility that someone else might get a wave, or drop in on his one. As the swell approached, his paddling and backward glances became almost manic, and the phrases spilt out at breakneck speed.

There was no doubt that he could surf, for he took the biggest of the three-wave set from a long way inside, got covered up, then came out to gather speed and work the face and lip down along to the beach.

A small spark of optimism half suggested that this might assuage the frenzy. But it was totally misplaced. Within three minutes he was back at the takeoff, and not just anywhere but right inside as if it were his position alone, babbling and spilling his siege mentality. Four waves later I'd seen enough. As I turned to paddle I heard someone say to him in a tired voice, 'Take it easy, mate, let's just take it easy.'

COUNTRY DREAM 2

The room was absolutely bare, its walls were white, and there were no windows. We were sitting on simple straight-backed wooden chairs, farmhouse chairs, just the two of us, and I was telling Sue about the hollow waves.

I began my description and leaned forward in a mock-tube crouch, arms cocked with fingers extended. As I did so, a silver translucent lip slipped over me. I was slotted in there, three metres back and totally enveloped looking out at Sue who sat on her chair listening to the description from further out along the wave.

I was aware of movement and a strange rumbling noise and golf-ball-sized droplets that fell in front of me.

As my description ended the lip slid back and I emerged into the whiteness of the room still seated in my chair.

There was no water anywhere on the floor of the room, and neither of us remarked at all on what had just happened. There was nothing to question.

TUESDAY DIARY SCRIBBLE

Departed tent early after light cup of tea, toast with heapings of butter and honey running together in a creamy spread — out through the bizarre twistings of the melaleuca grove, bark dripping wax-like from soft-skinned boughs that I'd seen in last night's moonlight — onto the sand and up along beach — small empty waves peeling down with airbrush-like softness cross-fusing at the edges with the light — left Carl beside tidal pool, tiny figure sitting, later just lying — gentle rides, small sections, sets and self synchronised at one point, each time I got back to the takeoff, next set was there waiting — morning arrival in camp from the west, truck hung with boards, fishing rods, chained spare tyres, jerry cans and kelpie, talked of 'big waves' and the coast last year. Seems if you get it pumping that first time, that's the way you'll carry it to the grave. 'Big waves', like 'You should have been here yesterday', or even 'an hour ago before the onshore got up' — afternoon impulse to try the big bluff down past the town, very peaky hollow with eight out, but spread out and good feeling. Ageing innocent fell into a couple. One that flashes like a beacon, wave crawling over me, sandy old lip lowering itself in slow motion out there in front of me, the exit altering shape all the time and then the whole thing drilling me, carrying me into waist-deep water and near collision with another guy. 'You gotta go for them every time,' he said when I asked if I'd hit him — tiny parts almost clichés now for some, but no matter, important thing is not to lose sight of them as they affect me. Can't accept responsibility for others and their loss of innocence or whatever it might be, easy now to go down the drain with everything that's floating around out there in the media. Symbols like words or paints only clothe the idea.

ONE OF THESE DAYS

The bird of paradise I realised fairly early in the piece, came in a variety of forms, and its landings more often than not were nebulous affairs that rolled up from within. A wisp. A feeling as you boiled the kettle after three hours in clean uncrowded waves, or listened to the notes of a lone tin whistle seeping across the crystal stillness of a creek bed.

Whatever shimmering dogmas lie at the heart of surfing lore, whatever half-expressed visions and fragments of cliché there are floating around, at some point it ultimately comes back to the mélange of personal perceptions and the receptiveness of the receiver. Like a vanishing point, or a landing spot. It could be either, or both.

If I had wanted it badly enough, I suppose it could have been some type of pilgrimage. A fantastic whirling thing that drew all experience into itself like some Siddhartha machine, journeying to the innermost limits of the surfing body, along the well-trodden tracks of the founding fathers with their endless nostalgia, and then beyond somehow in search of the Holy Grail, the final truth, returning in the best traditions of surf journalism with a set of ultimate findings, the perfect wave at a location never to be revealed, or a winner and some dollars.

But I'd never seen it in those terms, and besides, Handley had already indicated a possible direction from the kitchen of his hill home all that time ago. And those graves had clearly established that there's always another way.

Jeff knew that, but for him it was a Californian lesson that had still to impact on Australia in a major way. With his perforated eardrum plugged with yellow powder, cotton wool and grease ('The doctor said a month out but I wasn't passing this up'), he'd paddled out with unendingly good grace into a weekend insanity of six- to eight-foot barrels, along every lip of which the hordes were festooned and stroking in with never a care, every unspoken rule broken down and gone.

'Perhaps they're just desperate,' I'd said.

'But you wouldn't do it, I wouldn't do it,' he replied. And later, to the insincere 'sorry' of yet another drop-in, 'Don't give me that jazz, you're not sorry!'

There never was a watershed, not even a climax around which the whole thing pinned itself. Just a host of impressions, some perceptions, feelings that ranged across a spectrum and had no particular significance by themselves.

Settling down like a migratory bird at the end of its long flight was one part of it, at which point the waves didn't really seem to matter that much. They were there or they were not there, and the feeling was more of something bigger. A Chinese painting perhaps, where man is always subordinate to nature, infinitesimal in the total cycle, occupying but a tiny corner of an otherwise empty scene. I don't profess to know what it is in surfing that reaches deep inside of us, and to a lot of surfers it won't ever really matter at any rate. But there is a capacity for silence that each of us understands intuitively, and for me at least, surfing and the sea are the fastest ways to always get back to that quiet and balance.

The rest is really just a rustle at the edges.

Food for the Soul

The first traces of a soft North Coast dawn were stirring effortlessly along the eastern horizon that morning, as I pedalled my bicycle past Johnny Lim's grocery, and paused for breath where two vacant lots bordered the weathered timber walls of the fishermen's co-operative. In the gloom of the far distance I could just see the rock groynes of the river mouth, and beyond them the bar, with its long white sliver of breaking wave. There was a swell of some sort all right, and I was on my way to work.

Beside me, the creek was filling with floodlit prawn trawlers returning from a night's work, manoeuvring themselves to raft up alongside the Fish Board wharf. In spite of the heavy, incessant throb of diesel motors that hung in the air, the feeling was of a gentleness, a timelessness that the heat of the day would later burn off. At least that's how it seemed to me, and it always did, in those weeks just before the cyclone season kicked in and the big swells came back.

Across from Shanahan's Bridge, with its ornate wrought-iron work, the road forked, and I turned onto the rough verges of Dawson Street that ran inland for the best part of a kilometre alongside the rail yards. On my left the high-set old timber houses were for the most part still darkened, and several dogs barked as my wheels crunched past on the gravel. Here and there a strident male voice demanded silence. 'Git here, ya mongrel!' or something similar, cut through the air.

Early morning starts have never been a favourite of mine, and this one was no different. As the big peppercorn tree in the hotel yard materialised beside me, I swung off the seat to open the corrugated-iron gate. Maybe I should have been surfing? But I reasoned the river mouth and its waves would just have to wait till later in the day. A job's a job, and nothing lasts forever. This one would do until the cyclone season started, or I moved on. Besides, it wasn't all bad, the breakfasts were good, the barmaids were friendly, and there was always the free stubbie of stout at the end of a shift. 'Food for the soul', Harry the publican called it, and I never argued with that.

The Friend in Hand Hotel, with its Frangipani Bar, had never been what you would call one of the town's top watering holes. Some called it a 'faded beauty', but that assumed a glamorous past, which in fact it had never had. Others spoke of it as 'a bloodhouse on the edge of town', but that also was incorrect. Sure, there was a fight or two sometimes, and God knows I'd cleaned off enough blood from the toilet walls to set up a transfusion service. But like most drinking places, 'respectable' and otherwise, it had its own logic of social structure and pecking order. When they were understood and undisturbed, when respect was given and received, it all worked well, just like a boxing gym.

The multi-racial clientele comprised mainly domestics, cannery and rail workers, prawn fishermen and women, itinerants and pensioners living out their days in one of the many nearby boarding houses. They were a friendly, unpretentious crowd, for whom the racing and rugby results loomed large.

They were all drinkers, but one group, whom I privately called 'The Boys', were very serious about it. Pensioners for the most part, they would cluster every morning by the steel mesh doors in their grubby khaki shorts, tattered singlets, and thongs, their red faces ablaze from the ravages of lifetimes spent working and drinking in the full northern sun. If I didn't get those doors opened on the first knock of 10 a.m., they'd begin shaking the mesh bars and howling in unison. It was as if they were attending an exorcism, which in a way I suppose they were.

Once inside, they'd perch themselves on stools along the bar counter, each with a stubbie in a cooler, and there they'd sit. As yardman, my job entailed two shifts, 6 a.m. to 1 p.m., and 5 to 6 p.m. When I left in the evening they'd still be there, considerably the worse for wear, but invariably having solved many of the world's problems in a way that would put most politicians, the press, and the International Crisis Centre to shame.

In the gloom of that particular morning I propped my bicycle between the base of the peppercorn tree, and the rusted tin storage shed that held the leftover bar stools, the excess iron bedsteads and sideboards from the hotel rooms, and the empty kegs awaiting the brewery truck.

I then strode towards the back entrance of the Frangipani Bar. The door was ajar, which meant Harry was already up, and through the opening, lit by the weary yellow pallor of two fluorescent tubes, I could see on the far wall the picture of Vic Patrick in fighting stance. 'A Champion of Australia' the faded caption read.

Harry met me just as I stepped up into the doorway. He was wearing his dark blue and maroon check wool dressing gown, and it wasn't done up. Underneath were his pale pink and grey striped flannel pyjamas, tied by a cord at his waist and reaching down to just above his ankles. A pair of brown corduroy slippers covered his feet.

It was an outfit that always made him look vulnerable, yet at the same time totally at ease with the world. In truth, for the most part, that's how Harry approached things at 6 a.m. Even when drunks on a bender would show up in the dawn light to buy flagons of port, and threaten to kill him, he never let it worry him. 'They'll sleep it off,' he'd say, and invariably he was right. I'd see them at midday, passed out in the full sun on the grass beside the railway cutting. 'You surfers don't understand these things,' he would laugh.

But this particular morning Harry certainly wasn't at ease. As I came into the bar he scampered across to meet me, still clutching the stock sheet he used each morning to tally the night's drinking.

'You keep him talking, and I'll get the cops,' he whispered as he slipped past me through the door, and off up the back stairs that led to his living quarters on the hotel's first floor.

Over the time I'd been Harry's yardman, I'd seen a few fights, some alcohol-induced comas and collapses, a stabbing, a couple of attempted rapes, a certain amount of push and shove, and listened to a lot of shouting. So my only thought as Harry swept by was, 'Well, what have we got this time?' It became clear soon enough.

He was sitting on a stool, midway down the bar, more or less where the counter turned in a rounded U, and ran back on itself. From the far side of the room, and in that light, he didn't look like trouble to me, certainly not police trouble. I wondered if Harry had it wrong. Innocuous would have been the term I'd have settled on to describe that first impression.

He was of average size and weight, but with a dragged-down look that made him appear smaller than he was. A pair of dark trousers were held at his waist by a well-worn hand-tooled leather belt, into which was tucked a grubby white shirt. The sleeves of the shirt were rolled up above his elbows, and a series of badly faded and indistinct blue tattoos covered his forearms. He was wearing scuffed black leather shoes. His grey felt hat lay on the counter in front of him, beside a stubbie of beer, its dark blue band stained with an irregular line of sweat salt.

From the far end of the bar I started upending stools onto the counter, working my way down the line, to clear the area for sweeping, and then hosing out. Every day began like that. The tiled floor was a mishmash of butts, empty and partly full cigarette packets, spilt liquor, the odd broken glass, spittle, and coins. 'Any money you find on the floor is yours,' Harry had told me on my first day, 'what's left on the counter is mine.'

As I drew down the bar, the cause of Harry's early morning agitation became apparent. The stooped figure had hardly moved, or acknowledged my presence in any way. On the floor beside his feet was a battered suitcase, but on the bar in front of him, still partly wrapped in newspaper, but with enough showing to be obvious what it was, lay a twelve-gauge shotgun with a walnut stock.

I lifted up the stool beside him, and half turned, so that for the first time I was looking directly down on his dark hair, and the thin spot on top. 'Keep him talking,' Harry had said.

'How's it going mate?' I asked.

He glanced up at me, and then turned aside. 'OK,' was all he said.

They say that a man's character is his fate, and if that's true, then how often does his face carry his story? Often enough I'd say, and this face was one of those. For a start it carried a black eye and puffiness around the left cheek.

It was what might be called an Australian battler's face, of the type you see in press photos of crowds at football games in the 1930s, before substantial immigration and rising living standards started impacting on the general populace. It was also a world-weary face, for which things hadn't worked out in a long time, and might never have had a chance to work out. A certain amount of drinking was in there somewhere too. Rough, worn, tired and a bit pinched, it gave no real clue as to how old he might be. He might have been forty, but then he probably looked forty when he was twenty-five. Who knows?

'Just got into town?' I asked as I moved around him and started to work my way back along the remaining stools.

'Yeah. Drove in last night,' he said, 'and I reckon they'll be looking for me already.'

It was a cocky statement, but full of empty bravado. 'Had a bit of trouble with a ringer outside the Central,' he went on. 'Called me a dog and a no hoper. I fixed him up all right.' He tapped the partly covered shotgun on the counter. 'They see this and they shut up real quick,' he said.

I let it slide through without comment. 'So what happens next?' I asked.

He didn't look at me; in fact he didn't even look up from the counter.

'I'll just have a quiet little drink or two down here,' he half muttered, 'and then I'm gunna catch up with me missus. She's just down the road here a bit.' He paused and half-heartedly threw his hand in the direction of Dawson Street. 'She's got the little girl with her.'

I knew most of the houses he'd indicated and nearly every one of them had seen better days. Rusting car bodies, old refrigerators and washing machines littered their yards. It wasn't somewhere I'd have wanted my 'missus' to be, at least not for the long haul.

'I'm just gunna have a quiet little drink or two,' he went on, 'and then I'm goin' down there to shoot the bitch. She and her flash fuckin' friend. Last chance, no worries.' A hopeless chuckle broke from his mouth.

To be absolutely honest what he said didn't fully register with me. Harry had asked me to keep him talking, and that's what I was trying to do. I supposed that if he was going to have a 'quiet little drink or two' that in time the cops would arrive. But I didn't really know.

I wasn't exactly sure if talking was the best thing for him, or if it was likely to push him into action. There're two schools of thought on talking, aren't there? One says that if they talk about it they'll never do it; the other says that after the event everyone remembers all the times they said they'd do something and nobody took any notice. So what was it to be? I didn't know. I was just a surfer.

By now I had the bar stools up, the broom out, and had begun traversing the floor from one side of the room to the other, and back.

'Do you reckon that's the best thing to do?' I asked him.

'I dunno,' he said, 'but it's what I'm doin'. You can only take so much.'

For a moment he was quiet, as if doing a stocktake in his mind of everything he'd 'taken'. And then he just started to talk, more or less to himself, and there wasn't anything I had to say or do to keep it from coming. It just started to fall out of him.

'I could handle the arguments and the nagging,' he said. 'In fact at the start we used to laugh about them sometimes. But it all slowly changed, and I didn't realise what was happening. That's how it goes with women. You think it's one thing, but it turns out to be something else. The goalposts keep changing. That's what women do, they keep changing the goalposts.'

I'd heard the same lines plenty of times over the years, generally accompanied by an exasperated but good-humoured laugh. But this time there was no laugh, just a sadness, an admission that something had failed for him, and he didn't know why. In fact he'd probably never know, and the emptiness it left would never fill.

'I thought it was the money, and I signed up for every extra shift they offered at the mine,' he went on. 'God knows, I was raking the stuff in — overtime, penalty rates, danger money, away-from-home allowances, the lot. I gave her and the little girl a good life. But it was never good enough, never good enough.'

I knew what was coming. It stood out a mile, but I couldn't bring myself to say anything to stop the speeding train, to try and turn it around, and send it back up the line of time so that the whole thing would never happen. When I thought about it later, I realised that's probably how it had been for him.

'I was at work for weeks at a time,' he said, pausing to drink from his stubbie. 'Gone for weeks at a time. And after a while a few of the guys at the mine would say strange things to me, like, "Why not take the weekend off, mate, and get home?" or, "How's things with the missus?"

'For a fair while I never twigged what they were getting at. But they knew all right. In time everybody knew, but me.' He paused for a moment, swimming in the unfairness of it. 'And then I went home a day early, that time with the broken wrist, and there he was. Someone else in my home, sitting at my kitchen table, playing with my little girl, and poking my fuckin' wife.'

There was nothing I could say. I'd seen it coming in one form or another from the moment he first mentioned his 'missus'. There's a million versions of the same story floating around out there in bar rooms across the country, and every one of them has got two sides, but at 6 a.m in the Frangipani Bar that day I was only ever going to get one of them, and this was it. I didn't feel comfortable with this, men never do, but Harry had said, 'Keep him talking.'

'Well these things happen,' I offered, half trying to soften his hurt, to leach off the anger such as it was.

'Oh yeah, these things happen all right,' he said, reprising my words, 'and sometimes you get over it. You fix it up, you talk it out, and you think you've put it all together again, maybe even like it was at the start. And just when you're ready to put it behind you and get on with life, it happens again, and then again, and then again.

'Well, this time it won't be happening again. This time's the last time,' he said, staring straight ahead. 'Yesterday when I got back home after two weeks away, she's gone, done a bunk, left a note on the kitchen table and shot through. Just seven fucking words on a piece of white paper.'

He was silent for a moment, and then a sort of exasperated breath passed out from his mouth. 'I probably could've handled just that by itself, but she's taken the little girl with her too.'

I knew he was close to cracking, but I didn't know what to say. Men never do. One part of me was asking why wasn't I surfing; the other knew again what a thin veneer keeps us men going. It's a fragile thing and most of the time it doesn't bear too much talking about.

I looked across at him and fumbled for the right words. I don't think it really mattered to him whether I was there or not. He drained the stubbie and pushed it out in front of him. 'If she thinks she can do that to me on top of everything else, she's got another thing coming,' he said.

At that moment there was a shuffle at the back door. It was Harry, with 'Big' Bob Beaumont, one of the local coppers. They came in like part of a funeral procession, and Harry looked decidedly yellow around the gills.

Beaumont was leading. As he crossed the floor and reached the seated figure, he leaned across with his right hand and casually slid the shotgun along the counter, just as if he were wiping some crumbs away.

'It's a bit early to be thinking about things like this, isn't it?' he said. He then placed his left arm across the stooped shoulders of the figure next to him.

It was a good move, because it put him between the shotgun and its owner, and carried a feeling with it that things were under control.

'Why don't we go back to the station and have a bit of a talk about it?' he asked rhetorically, as if there were a choice involved.

The man stood up and looked at his suitcase. Beaumont motioned for him to pick it up.

'Before I go, can I give him something?' he said to Beaumont, and indicated me with a gesture of his head. The big policeman nodded.

The man put the suitcase on the bar counter and opened it. From on top of a pile of un-ironed work shirts and overalls he took out a well-used child's doll, of a type you might win in shooting galleries at country shows.

'Could you do me a favour, mate?' he asked. 'Would you take this for me and go down there, to the house on the corner, the one with the ute out front, and give it to the little girl.'

For a moment he held the doll in his hand, just looking down at it.

'I won it for her last year at the local rodeo,' he said, 'and I know she'd never mean to leave it behind. I used to tell her if she ever got lost, or left home without it, that I'd find her and get it back to her. She thinks I'm a hero.'

He passed it across to me, and for a second our eyes locked. I looked at him and nodded. 'Sure, mate,' I said.

There was a silence. Beaumont let him repack the suitcase and pick up his hat, then steered him to the door, gathering up the shotgun as he passed it.

They stepped down through the back door. Morning had

finally broken. The sun was fully up, and before long the brewery truck would be at the gate.

I looked at Harry. He seemed to be regaining some of his colour. 'Don't do that to me again,' I said with a wry smile.

'Oh, you take it too seriously,' he said. 'He wasn't ever going to do it. You surfers never see things as they really are. You live in a different world from the rest of us. You're always off-centre.'

He reached across the counter. 'Here, have a stout,' he laughed and twisted the top off a stubbie. He dropped it into a cooler and placed it in front of me. 'Food for the soul,' he said. It was just after 6.20 a.m.

When I knocked off later that day, I took the doll down to the house with the ute in front and placed it on the timber steps below the front verandah. Inside, I could hear a woman's voice and the sounds of a little girl playing. When she found it, I hoped she'd know her hero hadn't let her down.

Beaumont told us later that he'd taken the man back to the lockup, left him to sleep for a few hours, then put him in his car and told him to get out of town. A night or two afterwards, he'd thrown the shotgun into the creek, just up from Shanahan's Bridge.

Time Traveller

Four of us were cruising the coastal road down south, and that night we had set up camp just on dark in a tea-tree clearing, well off the track and below a headland that gave the bay its name. It was autumn and we all remembered later how quickly his figure had come out of the darkness and appeared in the firelight by the edge of our camp. 'Materialised' is the only word that gives the sense of how it happened. One moment there was just the four of us, and the next he was standing there. We didn't know where he'd come from; as far as we knew the place was deserted. And yet there he was.

Behind him were the sounds of the waves, magnified in the clean, crisp stillness of the night air. It's one of those high latitude, atmospheric things you sometimes get and it doesn't always mean the waves are big. Quite often it's just a state of the tide and the waves will be cracking on a half-exposed sand bank, with a sound out of all proportion to their size.

'How are you, boys?' he had said.

There were vague and somewhat non-committal murmurings of acknowledgment. Veiled thoughts of another freak about to lay it on us swirled through my untrusting brain. Not one of us wanted to be the one to extend even a half-decent welcome.

'Surf good today?' he'd asked, ignoring our indifference and stepping forward to where the fire threw yellow light in darts across his figure.

'Oh yeah ... Yeah, it was OK.' The murmurings were still lukewarm and uninviting, suspicious and stand-offish. But he seemed to ignore them and moved in closer to where the four of us clustered like moths in the benevolent glow of the flame.

He was old, but not that old. In fact his age was almost indeterminable, and when I think of him now it's only a sense that remains, a feeling of him, and not a lot of descriptive detail. His eyes had that clear look to them, a disturbingly reborn look that usually gives me the willies. They had a clairvoyance to them that suggested they remembered the future, if you know what I mean. Later, when we talked about him, none of us could remember anything about him but those eyes and his whitish hair.

'Mind if I share a bottle?' he had asked, swinging a three-quarter-full brandy bottle into view. 'I'm camped up there a bit,' he gestured with his hand, 'gets quiet and I like to talk a bit every so often.'

He sat down next to Steve, who looked decidedly uncomfortable and confessed later that he thought the 'old fella' had his eye on him.

For a time the talk was general and the old man just listened, passing his bottle out whenever a cup was emptied. Inevitably we got on to the best spots and the best breaks and the best shapes. The old man asked us how many spots we'd surfed at and how many waves we reckoned we'd ever ridden.

The estimates were at best just stabs in the dark; someone even attempted to work up an average for waves caught per session per day surfed per year for so many years. The result was general laughter, until the old man quietly said, 'I know a guy who's surfed every spot from Noosa to Bells to Red Bluff, and everything in between, the Islands, Mexico, Indo, Europe, you name it, Africa, South America, wherever. If there's been a wave worth picking up, this guy's been there.'

There were lighthearted murmurs and somebody said, 'You'd better tell us about him.'

'Oh, there's a lot I could tell you about him,' the old man said, 'but I don't know that you'd listen. The bloke I'm talking about remembers every wave he's ever ridden, he can give you the exact number at each spot and their size.'

There were hoots of good-natured laughter, and cries of 'Oh yeah! Give us more'. But the old man just went on as if nothing were happening.

'The bloke I'm talking about has ridden everything from 18-foot solid redwood planks to composite-material body boards,' he said. 'He's surfed with his body, he's ridden every known piece of wave equipment ever devised and more — planks, malibus, shortboards, skis, kneeboards, mats, hand blades, sticks of every configuration, Tear Drops, Pigs, Stubbies, Trackers, Sideslippers, White Kites, Pocket Rockets, Stingers, Lazer-Zaps, all of that stuff and more. Round tails, pintails, swallow tails, single fins, twin fins, thrusters, reverse sheer, pronounced sheer, flat bottoms, flyers, concaves, double concaves, V-bottoms, channel bottoms, rolled rails, down rails, keel fins, four fins. The lot. Everything. Absolutely everything.'

As the laughter rolled over us we looked at one another and a few eyebrows were raised. What had we got ourselves into? It was outrageous, but somewhere at the edge of it was a disturbance, something not quite right, a feeling that ran into a dead end and finished with a 'What if?' Well, none of us knew.

'Does he ride big waves?' I asked, half in jest, trying to keep things moving along, as the others just laughed.

'Yeah, he does,' was the answer. 'You remember this tow-in guy who claimed the other day he'd taken the biggest wave ever ridden? Out at Jaws or one of those places, they reckoned it was 50 or 60 foot.'

We all nodded. The papers had been full of it.

'You won't want to believe this,' the old man went on, 'but my fella was out there the night before, alone in the moonlight. And he didn't need to be towed in! You all know every seventh wave is supposed to be a bit bigger than the rest, and that the mathematicians have worked out the odds of really big waves as being something like one in two billion. Well, the night before that guy was towed in at Jaws, the odds came up out there . . . and my man was there!

'He told me later they were coming through at 60 foot plus when this monstrosity came in out of the dark. He heard it first, and then felt the movement of the wind around him shift and swirl under the influence of the approaching waveface. He put it at well over 100 feet and said his takeoff was a free fall. By the time he made the drop and cranked into his bottom turn the tail of the board was glowing red and his wake had vapourised into white steam.

'He shot back up the face with such speed that his re-entry was in the air 25 feet above the lip. You hear what I'm saying — 25 feet above the lip on a 100-foot plus wave! That's some reo by anyone's reckoning! Another plunge and the board was becoming too hot to stand on. By the time he got to the shoulder and off it, the glass on the board had melted, and the foam blank was charcoal. He had to swim in, and his only disappointment was that no one was there to see it.

'But you know, a day or two later there was a report tucked away in the bottom corner of page three of the *Honolulu Times* where some kook reckoned he'd seen a red vapour trail two nights before, moving about in what he thought was the sky, about 70 feet above the big surf breaking on the outer reefs. The article reported that no one believed him. It went on to say that the local police chief "suspected drugs had a part to play in the observations" and that the police "would be making an example of him".'

The laughter that greeted this part of the old man's story drowned out the sound of the waves breaking behind the sand dunes. But the old man seemed unfazed. He had a benign-looking half-smile on his face that suggested an indulgence.

'Has he ridden any tubes?' someone eventually asked, choking on the effort to get it out.

'This guy has been in barrels big enough to fit a house,' the old man said. 'He's been further back in them than anyone, and stayed in there long enough to have a birthday. He's gone into tubes at one beach on a Saturday afternoon and come out Sunday morning somewhere up the coast. And once again nobody realises what he's done, because they don't know where he's come from.'

By now we'd all nearly choked on our brandy and as I reached forward for the bottle I noticed the old man staring at us intently, his eyes catching the glow of the coals so that two pinpoints of red were set beneath the white hair. His indulgent smile had gone.

'You people are too full of yourselves,' he said, his voice tinged with a moral touch that at the time I attributed to the brandy, but certainly didn't care about. 'You think you're the only ones that can do it. I'll tell you this, and you can take it or leave it, but my time is all the time, and whatever you do it's already been done and will be done again and again and again.

'The bloke I've told you about,' he went on, 'was playing in the surf at Kealakekua Bay in 1779 when Captain Cook arrived. In fact the only picture or photograph of him that I know of is in the painting done by Cook's artist John Webber. It shows the English ships arriving at Kealakekua and the Hawaiians paddling out to meet them. If you look carefully among all the canoes and swimmers you'll see a solitary figure on a surfboard. That's my man.

'There's been an awful lot of surfers since then and a lot of stuff written about them. But never a word about my man. Have you ever wondered why?' He paused, and then went on. 'Because he's a spirit and they can't catch a spirit. Look at what they present now as surfing.' And he rattled off a string of names — some of them people, some of them companies, that grouped collectively constitute the commercial reality of contemporary surfing.

As he did so, I reached again for his brandy bottle. It had no label, and the amber richness of the liquid splashed about the clear glass. It was only as I replaced the bottle by the old man's legs that I realised it was still three-quarters full, just as it had been an hour before when he'd first stepped into the light of our fire. But in that hour five of us had been drinking steadily from it.

I heard his voice, by now a lot softer, and realised that some of the others were no longer really listening.

'There's a lot of ego out there,' he said. 'Sure, some of them are good, but they'll go and others will come. My man doesn't lay it all out there just because he can ride a wave or two.' He paused amid the laughter and with what I thought could have been self pity added, 'He's got too much style for that sort of thing.'

'But we all need some recognition,' I said to him. 'We all need somebody to know and care.'

He turned towards me, and lowered his voice so that the others who were still laughing could not hear.

'You're right there, son, and you're my recognition. You're my man. In a few years they'll know what I was talking about.' He gestured at the others. 'Don't worry, the penny will drop. One day they'll remember what I've been talking about and they'll know that the things I've said were done, have been done. Time does all things.'

I guess the alcohol had slowed me down, because I let him wander off into the darkness with his three-quarter-full brandy bottle as friendlessly as he had arrived. For a time the others didn't even know he'd gone. The next morning none of us could find his camp and we wondered had it ever happened.

But now, years later, every one of us remembers the stories in the same way.

Sometimes we laugh and sometimes we don't.

Seasons

SUMMER

Summer is often a thing of the mornings, snatched in the quiet that precedes the afternoon southerly. It's expansive and seemingly never-ending, like a long drawn out bottom turn. It's a peacock tail spread out to dazzle and confuse with its thousand eyes, flashy and strutting all at the same time, like a contest re-entry, board thrown casually this way or that, as much in the air as the water.

Summer is a time to take risks — there is nothing that can happen, nothing that cannot happen. It's a fair wind rustling the casuarinas with that bittersweet northern moan, coarse sand and broken shell underfoot, an island isthmus and the long extended seaway stretching into the distance, with its million promises pushing deep into 'the blue desert'.

What languages are spoken out there, I wonder, where the swells are born and roll unridden and unimpeded for thousands of miles? Summer song perhaps? More likely island voices, caught midway through a Christian hymn with its sweet by and by, their nasal melody sweeping down from a white weatherboard church, past a stand of wind-brushed palms and out across a beach, fusing in part-perfect union with the ever-constant rumble of an unrideable six-foot wave rolling across the reef fringing their lagoon.

Summer is no gilded cage.

AUTUMN

Autumn is an obsession. It's the time of harvest, a time of transition for those who allow the seasons to work their subtlety.

Autumn is . . . where? A 1954 figure now half lost in the passage of time and the blown spume of yet another giant swell. A tiny speck dancing spider-like and alone, seen by those on the shore to be 'out the back somewhere', solitary and lost, glimpsed briefly rising, then gone forever in the noise and the foam of that broken sea. Someone saw him take off in the fading autumn light of that late afternoon, his body balancing those surfing keystones of stance, gravity, speed and ultimately survival.

He passed from sight, re-appeared, then passed from view again . . . forever lost 'down there', way out where the finger of an outstretched hand directs the gaze towards a headland. It was called a 'surfing accident' and much later the magazines recorded his years of surfboard design and riding as 'the only period of true innovation the sport has endured'. Strange, isn't it?

Well, in the high southern latitudes autumn can have that same dour feel, as if a descent into something has begun. Wood smoke stirs the senses and the night wind lays about you like life and death. Mauve is the colour I seem to remember best, glimpsed as it falls over an evening landscape, the road from Bells reaching up and into the ironbarks, the swell a procession from far out to sea.

WINTER

'It's the ones that come through wide you've got to watch out for,' I heard myself say one winter Saturday. 'Most times now when I try to make the drop there's got to be at least a sixty-forty chance of somewhere to go.'

Winter for me is that great grey resting place of vision and dream and half-caught remembrance. It's a southern seascape peopled with ghostly black figures, faces drawn white with cold, bloodless and transparent, forever trying to make that transition from land to sea to land, from something-or-other to surfer and back again.

Winter is both a finishing point and a starting point.

It's a coastal strip, marram grasses ablaze with wind, rustling like wildfire, shaking and throwing forever here and there and here, with the Strait a tortured tumbling mass of dirty brown storm sea, alive, rippling and thrusting, its surface a pulse of driven fury.

Winter is also an empty sea.

It's a vision, but altogether a lot more liquid, like a descent held forever at just short of arm's length, of paddling in late or not hard enough, with the drop down a broken lift cable, hands flung up above the head, the instant passing before me as those on the beach might see it. Separate, detached, falling, and totally free.

SPRING

'Days lengthen, winds strengthen' is the adage, but there's more to it than that. God knows, there are few journeys' ends for any surfer worth their salt, but spring must hint of something.

It's that unexpected offering caught when the rest of the world was doing something else . . . well, it seemed that way for an hour at least! Leaving the rock shelf in the purple–pink dawn, light slowly seeping across the land like a hesitant lover. Those first chill washes smooth with a noise that allowed just a brief touch of the inner rhythms . . . and the laughter later when the others came. 'How long have you had this to yourself?' they asked. 'I've always been just a flash in the pan,' I replied.

Spring is a tidal thing of ebb and flow, point and counterpoint, a hint of something more enduring perhaps. The view from spring for me has always had a sense of distance. It's a long ride to Damascus, but in spring I sometimes seem to know where I'm going and why, and what I've left behind.

Spring images are clean, their flavour a sweet thing caught in sounds like 'crystal' or 'country'.

A landfall at dawn on that beautiful shore.

The Graduate

The beginning was simple enough. A half-defined feeling, fertilised by billboard images, a few DVDs and the thought that maybe he could score with some of those ladies at the pub. The niche was there all right. It was cool, he was sure of that, and he figured he was just the guy to fill it.

A week and three back editions of *Tracks* later, he arrived in Torquay for his surf lesson. It was 9 a.m. on a Saturday morning and because of the size of the swell the lesson had been shifted to the shelter of the coast north of Point Danger. They called it Cosy Corner. What a breeze, he thought. It was 11 a.m. when he graduated and the world was his oyster. He was a surfer and he didn't give a shit what the instructor had said about taking it easy, rips and currents, levels of experience, respecting the ocean, or anything else. He went up to the Plaza and bought his first board and wetsuit.

It was early afternoon when The Graduate arrived at Bells. There was a fair crowd out, and the remnants of a murky cloudbank scudded off before a light northwesterly.

Even from the clifftop he knew they were big. But it still looked straightforward. A pristine swell on which tiny black-suited figures winged and soared their way shoreward. The adrenaline started. This was his place. He was cool.

A quick change and the cliff descent began. Beside the steps were three rocks, set in the ground with small aphorisms chiselled into the stone. *Respect yourself* the first one said; *Respect each other* the second. What a load of bullshit, he thought as he passed by the third without bothering to read it. The stream of figures around him now carried him down, as if he were part of a team moving out on to a sports arena. It was just as he'd imagined it.

He paused at the beach. Sea level. The perspective from here was different, but it was too late to turn back, there were others following. His niche was still there, but now he was uncertain.

The shore break was something he hadn't considered. Timing. A frantic dash, a leap and paddling, paddling, foam washing before him, following the others with the dawning of a thought deep inside that he'd have to work out a return routine in an hour or two . . . or whatever.

For a time he stroked his way seaward, his senses leaping to the thousands of options pressing forward for quick decision. By some miracle of which he was totally unaware, he made it out between sets. He edged northeast to stay outside the break, then sat up for the first time to take it all in.

The action still lay across from him, over there where the surfers sat waiting. His confidence was returning. Perhaps he could still find that niche and he was sure there were ladies back there in the car park watching, just waiting to see him take off.

He paddled across to what he assumed was the takeoff area. Just as he allowed himself a moment of contemplation, something moved at the corners of his vision and wild whoops came from the figures around him. Even before he clearly saw the set he sensed his time had finally come. They were big. Far bigger than he had expected and they came in, rumbling and gnashing with a hissing sound he had never heard before, nor imagined that waves could make. There were three of them. Heavy. Thick and grey. Somewhere on those sloping surfaces he hoped he'd find that groove.

He let the first two through and was appalled at the lift that accompanied the climb to the lip. At the same time, somewhere to the side and below him he was aware of a movement, and a white wake scarred the waveface. The third was his. Something told him he couldn't let it pass or there might never be another one, ever. He turned, and not even daring to look around him as his surf school instructor had told him, clawed and scratched his board into movement.

It came from behind as relentlessly as death itself. An upward incline, a lift, and the beginnings of forward movement and speed. Just as his shoot began, something else pressed forward from beside him to the left, something he hadn't really thought too much about. It was another surfer, lifting up off the bottom and heading to where The Graduate hung caught in the lip. 'Fuck off!' the surfer screamed as he wheeled inches from the nose of The Graduate's board and took off down into the valley below.

For a split second The Graduate hung suspended, his future laid out in front of him. In his mind each stage revealed itself with an awful clarity. He sensed rather than felt the terrible plunge forward, with its promise of oblivion. When it came over him, it was the heaviness of it that impressed him more than its violence. He surfaced breathless beside his board.

Shaken, he paddled to sea seeking a resting place, a sanctuary free from people's anger and the need to make decisions. A place to lick his wounds and somehow get it all back together. He made for a spot well out from the takeoff point. It looked peaceful and he figured that when he was ready he'd move back in and make another play. Scarcely had he begun to paddle when he heard again the whoops of the pack and saw the lifting on the horizon. Nemesis and the Midnight Special had rolled into one, and were coming through wide and fast.

Instinctively he knew they'd close out on him and there was nothing he could do. He slid from his board, pushed it aside and watched half-fascinated as the wall lifted and curled above him. He didn't even try to dive, and as it picked him up and took him down, day became night and his whole existence a matter of getting air. It was the power that shocked him. That, and the endless rumbling, the clawing and struggling to get back to the surface.

A second wave followed the first, with another behind that. He knew he was in trouble and somehow the scene with its ladies and everything else had faded a bit.

As the third wave passed and the terrible boiling receded and released him, he emerged faint and gasping. The sea about him resembled a snowfield, or the inside of a washing machine. Bubbles and foam, and heads and boards littered the surface as far as he could see.

That was it. He'd call it a day. Get ashore and try to figure it all out. He lay on his board gulping great breaths of air, periodically spitting and belching the last remnants of water from his stomach.

The paddle in came to assume the proportions of a voyage and he stared in disbelief at the impartial almost serene faces of those paddling out past him. Waves and broken water carried him in and along the coast towards the Winkipop Button. By a supreme effort he arrived just beyond the shore break, two-thirds of the way along Bells Beach. Across the flecked surface he could see the sanctuary of the steeply shelving sand. Between him and the beach lay a chasm, a purgatory he knew would extract the final toll from his limp and aching body. The true extent of the ordeal ahead of him now dawned. For a moment he baulked behind the break, postponing the disaster he foresaw with a terrible clairvoyance.

The water was thick with coarse sand, its surface white with froth, and unsettled, possessed of a movement like a river. He made his approach on the back of one wave, and for a time it went well. The wave stood up, dumped in front of him, then licked up the beach and began its surge back, dragging sand and stones in its wake.

His progress suddenly ceased and as his arms flailed uselessly, he felt himself drawn back and up into the clutches of the inevitable next wave. Quite suddenly the sand was below him and all the pieces fell into place. It was all so preordained, like life and death, black and white.

As he fell forward, to be driven face first into the sand, then rolled and buffeted and bounced and punched by the abrasive sea, he knew that he'd somehow crossed a frontier, but into exactly where or what he no longer knew or cared. He emerged from the foam to stagger and claw his way up the steeply shelving shoreline. The water clutched and clawed and dragged at his body and legs. It picked him up and sucked him back into its maelstrom, and then repeated the whole process anew, before depositing him again in knee-deep water. He fell, then rose, his face an anguished mask, one side lacerated, the other a ghastly white. Behind him, trailing from his legrope, was the lower half of his brand new board.

It was some time before The Graduate was able to walk along the beach to the steps and begin the slow ascent to the car park. His breath had returned, but his limbs were jelly, and he didn't care what the people on the clifftop above him thought. As he slowly climbed one step at a time, three fresh-faced black-suited figures passed down beside him. 'Have a good one, mate?' the first of them asked. The Graduate didn't reply. As the last of the figures slipped by, he saw for the first time the third of the stones with its chiselled message. The one he hadn't read on the way down. *Respect the ocean* it read.

In the Red Corner

Former world featherweight champion Sandy Saddler once said of boxing: 'It's hard work on the way up and it's hard work on the way down.' There are many surfers who box, but not a lot of boxers who surf. It's that sort of activity, and a serious commitment to what might be called 'the boxing life' runs surfing a very distant second.

I think it was George Foreman who called boxing 'show business with blood', and he wasn't wrong. Professional surfing prides itself on its 'man on man' contest formula, but if it seriously wanted to run close to boxing's notion of man on man it would send the pros out in heats of ten and forget the notion of priority. Every wave would then be ridden, and all sorts of things would be happening in all sorts of places, all of the time.

Whatever yellow brick road the commercialisation of surfing has taken, with its all-pervasive 'branding' now creeping inexorably outwards towards tea bags and tampons, it remains relatively innocent, and has yet to uncover its version of Don King.

Some lunatic called boxing 'the sweet science'. I'd say the person who coined that term had obviously not been hit around the head while listening to a crowd baying for his blood, because when that happens there's nothing 'sweet' about it at all.

But it is a science, and like surfing certain immutable laws underpin its every move. In the hands of its top practitioners, just as with surfing, it can cross that border into art form, where the laws of line or balance or rhythm are given interpretation by the individual.

In boxing, as in surfing, and indeed many other things, style counts for a lot. Names become synonymous with certain ways of doing something, with a line taken, a body angle, or an attitude. Think of some names and what comes to mind? Tom Carroll. Barry Michael. Kelly Slater. Johnny Famechon. Gerry Lopez. Oscar de la Hoya. Mark Richards. Kostya Tszyu. The list is endless, but there's always something there and a lot of the time it's indefinable, just a feeling.

In boxing there are two places where you can look good — in the ring and out of the ring. But only one place counts. Is surfing the same? A lot of people are world champions in front of the mirror or the speedball or the heavy bag. What ultimately and only counts in boxing is what goes on 'up there', 'in there', or whatever you like to call it. And it involves heart.

The first thing you quickly realise in boxing, if you hadn't before, is that you are totally and literally on your own. You sometimes get it in surfing, when you realise you're in a situation at the extremity of your ability, and beyond, be it six-foot, twelve-foot, or worse.

Nothing ever alters that essential truth of boxing. When you climb into that ring, under the bright white lights, you've left the crowd behind in a way the average surfer never does. Naturally it introduces an element of fear. Nobody really talks about it, but it's there just the same. It's like standing on the beach when it's big and wondering will you ever get out in one piece, and if you do will you ever get back in. How about a Hawaiian outing, where you enter the water late afternoon at the upper level of your size experience? As darkness nears you realise the swell is rising quickly and is now well above what you've ever ridden before.

Cus D'Amato, the man who first tapped Mike Tyson's terrifying early talent, always recognised the presence of fear in boxing. He believed it was there for the first fight, and still there for the hundredth fight. But if the boxer was to survive, D'Amato believed, well before a hundred fights he would develop enough discipline to learn to live with it. Is that what we do with big waves? Find our limits, learn to live with our fears, and tell near-drowning stories?

Boxing mirrors life in a way that surfing never does. Surfing is optimistic. Boxing can be, but often at the end it's bleak and full of lost opportunities. The surfer is lucky in a way that the boxer never is. Even into old age the surfer can hope that tomorrow will be six foot and offshore. What can the boxer look to in the same way? Most boxers and surfers spend a portion of their time in the past. But in his heart the surfer is still heading somewhere that the boxer can't really go.

Boxing can break your heart as quickly as look at you. It'll draw you up and spit you out faster than you can say 'Sugar Ray Robinson'. The boxer and the competition surfer share at least one common ground. It can all be so terrifyingly insubstantial. The narrowest of margins can be the difference ultimately between the scrap heap and glory.

But the boxer carries a far heavier load with him and some of it works like this: when he's not fit the promoter will ring and want him at short notice; when he is fit they never ring, or his scheduled opponent drops out at the last minute and a replacement can't be found; weights can come askew in the blink of an eye; win a few fights and suddenly he's in at a level above where he wants to be; lose a few and suddenly he's easy pickings for some up-and-comer; they tell him he's in with someone who couldn't bruise a grape, but how do they know that and why are they telling him in the first place? At the finish of it all he can find himself back in a change room without so much as a hand basin. In Melbourne some years ago boxing was promoted in the Dog Pavilion of the Showgrounds. What would most surfers know of these things?

The surfing gym is a place of sunshine, open air, light and laughter. The boxing gym is a netherworld, where sunlight is almost unheard of and certainly not valued. It's all figures moving this way and that, stepping inside, stepping outside, going under, slipping and sliding, getting in and getting out.

Some of them are lifers, others will come and go. Some with the moves, and some with never a hope in hell.

The thing with sparring is to find a level you're both happy with; a level where you each get something out of it. If you're in with someone good, there's always the paralysing uncertainty as to just how hard he will want to go. If you don't watch out it can freeze you up so you're just waiting for him to go into action and hoping that you'll weather the storm.

The figure in front of you is always moving, this way and that, in and out, up and down, and you're doing the same. You're looking to pick up on a rhythm in his movements, to get one of your own going and set your punches off that, rolling them out of your body. Lots of people can throw two punches. It's combinations that count, and they're all about balance, rhythm and timing.

As with surfing, the important thing is to find your own style and let that define you. People can tell you things, show you all sorts of moves, but in the end you have to reach inside to find out which part of it is really you, and go with that.

At the end of the day surfing and boxing come together as focus and intensity. Making the drop on a big one or slipping inside a heavy one with a combination ready to fire require a certain focus. The rest is adrenaline.

Cus D'Amato once said of the boxer: 'Knowing what he goes through, the very act of climbing into the ring stamps him as a person of courage and discipline.'

To be a surfer and have that same thing said about you would be good enough for me.

Jack the Wandering Albatross

It was early on a November morning when Jack the Wandering Albatross lurched to his feet. A fresh westerly wind was blowing and the grass tussocks beside his nest were rippling and alive with movement.

Almost a year earlier Jack had hatched from a single white egg his mother had laid. At first his parents had taken turns to stay with him, sitting over him and protecting him with their bodies. But as he grew bigger, and his soft downy covering changed to dark brown and white feathers, they came less and less. Jack would sit hunched and huddled through winter nights and days, with the snow and the hail and the roar of the west wind whipping around him.

Just when he thought he had been forgotten, his mother or father would fly in with his food of fish and squid. But now that he could stand and waddle and stretch his wings, they hardly came at all. It was as if they were telling him something had changed.

For some days he had stood in the grass of the hillside with the other young birds, flexing his wings this way and that, up and down, in and out. But the feeling had not been right. He knew he was not ready for whatever it was he was meant to do.

Each night he would squat beside the small heaped mound of grass and mud that had been his nest and silently stare into the darkness, waiting, just waiting. For a long time it was like this, and nothing happened.

But that November morning was different. A wind had come in during the night and as he listened to it freshening and felt its buffeting, something wonderful happened. He couldn't say exactly what it was, but he knew everything had somehow changed. He couldn't wait for the light to break to find out what it was.

Soon after dawn Jack stood facing the wind, his large webbed feet spread wide to take the rocking of his body. The wind smoothed his feathers. From the clifftop he could see the endless lines of swell stretching out across the sea below him and the white caps of the tumbling, breaking seas atop them. A flock of petrels circled and wheeled, their cries carried away in the wind.

Far out across the ocean, at the very edge of his sight a tiny white speck moved against the grey skyline. It was another wandering albatross, lifting to the wind, then dropping in a long drawn-out glide down the swell lines like a surfer, rising and falling to the swirls of wind that wafted from the wavefaces. At that instant Jack knew what the feeling inside him meant.

Shuffling forward he unfolded his wings and twisted and tilted them to meet the wind surge that swept about him. Leaning forward, he began to push his body down the slope of the hill. His first steps caught in the grass, and once he fell forward clumsily onto his chest. He rose to his feet and pushed off again. The slope began to get steeper and he was rushing faster and faster. Draughts of wind pushed up the hill caressing his feathers, lifting and lowering his body at the same time. As he spread his great wings wide, he became aware of a force taking hold of him from inside.

Suddenly, the slope ended at a cliff. The land fell away below him to the black rocks and the tumbling sea. Before he could even think about it and make things right, the momentum of his headlong plunge took him over the edge and out . . . out . . . out into the air!

Jack's flight had begun, and it was his alone.

It would be some years before Jack would again return to the land. During this time, like other albatrosses, his feathers would change to adult white and his fantastic surf wanderings would cover the waters of the world below Australia and New Zealand and the desolate and barren Cape Horn, to the edges of Antarctica itself. He would become a true maritime voyager, diving and soaring, lifting and wheeling, surfing his way over the waters of that great southern sea.

Roadsong

A MAP OF THE MIND

The signs have always been there, dreamtime clear, like tidal swirls at the base of a channel beacon, or the Braille-like indentations on the index arm of my sextant. Sometimes they resemble an Indonesian martial gesture, an inclination of a finger or a wrist, an arch from the ankle to the hand running through the spine, a direction indicated. Signposted. The ocean or the sea . . . the ocean and the sea.

Roadsong is about setting out somewhere with an only partly grasped notion that some things you find out for yourself away from home. Gentle, imperceptible feelings like the brush of a feather, that the time has come to cast off the lines and let the wind call the tune . . . the road and the water will work their own sweet therapies.

Early amber-morn half-light house departures, breakfast bowls clutched tight . . . like landfalls at dawn alive with promises and half-heard stories from other times . . . lines on a roadmap etching their blackness coastwise, thin and spidery to pencilled asterisks that someone has made to guide you . . . 'second turn right, below dairy, sou'west swell, winds north through west' . . . the instruction 'if it goes south', with an arrow annotated at a headland, and in your head the remembrance of a story you were told as the arrow was marked in, of twelve-foot waves with paper thin walls stacked up six lines deep. If it happened once it can happen again!

Is that how it goes at eighteen or twenty-eight or even fifty-eight? Expectations still out of control like any fourteen-year-old? Yes! Looking at the lines of yet another weather map . . . isobars and pressure systems, fronts travelling east, energy sources and the final knowledge that the time is only ever now and that sometimes the two might just become one . . . lines on a roadmap, lines on a weather map. Waves!

THE LIST

Albanian cognac

Gas bottles, water cans

clothes

2 spare legropes

jaffle irons

wetsuits

6'1" twinny shaped by Ross with red deck ('as red as the blood he shed for us')

7'2" yellow pintail shaped by visiting Californian

chewing gum

2 books: The Executioner's Song *and* Evangelism Inc.

2 fence palings for traction if bogged in mud or sand

note with phone number, 'if things go bad he might be able to help' telegram 'Bus arrives 10pm. Cheers Chris.'

Newspaper clipping with photo of ex-US Secretary of State Al ('Strangelove') Haig

List of names scribbled on back of cafe menu headed 'Oz Roll Call' as follows: Jimmy Carruthers, Dolly Dyer, Arthur Rylah, Pelita, Dirty Dick Raines, Lorraine Crapp, 'Chicken' Smallhorn, Brian of Brian's Speed Shops, Captain de Groot, Smokey Dawson

There were no surfers listed in the Oz Roll Call.

MESSAGES IN BOTTLES

Roadsong . . . strange lights in the sky at the eye's edge, fingering down and shimmering, mystic, wonderful, like Tennyson's Excalibur, leading off through the tundra of tangled vegetation and limestone-patterned rock ways. Feelings that a million things might happen on the roadsong and no one need ever know, so we left bottles with messages in them for people to find. One message said 'Fornication ain't no great sin', scribbled on a page and left in the empty Albanian cognac bottle, on a clifftop above a fast-peeling left. Message in a bottle.

Roadsong is knowing that with all the things that can be said, 'The List' says damn near everything. It's like a pulse beating back inside, and to which all the other things have attached themselves, telling you very clearly that it's going to take more than religion to save you.

Days and nights on the road, or at sea out beyond the islands and headlands of the coast. Slowly rising and falling. Nights alive, a full moon, silver flights of fancy, with streaked skies and the gentle blink-blink of a lighthouse. Barometer falling. 'It's times like this,' you hear yourself saying, 'that I wonder if we shouldn't pull in somewhere and get a handle on this weather.' But you don't.

The road can tell you a million things on where you've been, vibrations always there just waiting to be picked up. Polynesian navigators, someone said, could lie on the floor of a voyaging canoe and pick up wave vibrations through the wood . . . landfalls, eastern light dappling the sea far out there.

Roadsong is the red rust rattle of a '72 station sedan, flashes of colour and snatches of conversation from a South Coast petrol station proprietor looking at the surfboards tiered up from the roof.

'We should never have got out of Vietnam, you know,' he'd said out of the blue, all the while looking at me for some sort of response. He pronounced Vietnam as *Veetnam*. 'Johnson lost his nerve, and then Nixon . . . well I said the first time he was elected "that man's soft in the centre", and look what happened to him. Nixon . . . oh, jeeze,' he'd scoffed. I said maybe he was right, but I was just glad it was over and everybody was home again.

Roadsong is a meridian encircling a state of mind, a ritual of expectation . . . back seat earphones, bleached bones and sailors' ghosts, almost a circus feel, wondering what Bruce Springsteen means by 'the price you pay', and if all this movement is actually taking you to a surfable wave . . . pillows without pillow cases, the bold tartans inside a sleeping bag all thrown about a confused back seat.

Short-morning Australian store stops, out there lounging beneath the gently curved verandah, windows full with the ancient and timeless ads of that other age, for ice creams, headache powders and biscuits. Beyond the store door, the road dropping down close by, across a river flat with its dried timber bridge, stands a line of sand hills. If your hunches are right and your wind senses attuned, the flawless waves of an enlivened ocean are behind those sand hills. Roadsong ends. Anywhere. Nowhere. Everywhere. With hot cross buns dripping butter.

SOUTHERN CLIFFTOP

The experience . . . a quality of light morning and night. Figures standing staring out to sea, southern grey line squalls scudding by overhead, and cumulonimbus clouds at the horizon's edge . . . clifftop surveillances . . . grey ponderous waves or soft sunlight high-latitude silver–green peelers. Clifftops, flat rocks, beaches, sand squeaking underfoot, rock rubble at a cliff base . . . a hand, its wrist encircled with a silver bracelet, proffered its offering of periwinkle shell broken to intricate form, limpet shells and the sculptured wastes of a thousand storms.

Piles of dunnage whitening, caught amongst the rocks, washed up at the base of the sand hills and into the mouths of the coastal creeks.

I knew of a beach once where the surfers used dunnage to build a shack for themselves. From the door of the shack through a gap in the sand hills in front of you, an extremely hollow right-hander would peel for hours at a time if everything was OK, and on one occasion they rolled across like that for four days on end. The townspeople eventually burnt the hut down because 'it didn't have a permit'. The stumps are still there now in the marram grass, but everything else has changed. The banks have gone. It now works left from up near the Surf Lifesaving Club.

WAVES

Moments clear in the mind leaving the shore, slipping out into the day's first waves, water golden from the early sun, amber spray, sharp-scented ozone bubbles of foam popping and bursting beside you, or skin-dried salty afternoon launch outs, with cream whitened nose and eyebrows hung with fine white sea crystals ... launching out to what? Well, four things at least.

A peak pulling down past you, as you sit watching a figure slash its way down the line, vigorous cutting movements, deeply dug turns, rail-drawing fins lifting clear, and foam streaming astern in a speed line, arms and legs in total movement, down around and up to where a fantail of foam throws its sculptured pattern across the mind's eye, momentary disappearance, then the figure seen from behind and the realisation that a lot of those turns were taking place above the water.

The figure of some twelve-year-old caught frozen in under a lip, backhand on the way back up, z-tracked foam in the wake, body angle all arched to pivot, spine twisted to release torque, poised to unleash the barely makeable and certainly unjudgeable.

The contest circuit will forever beckon, but the ultimate expression of what it attempts to quantify and classify is something that will forever take place somewhere else, on a beach with no banners, by some loose-limbed kid for whom there are no limits.

A fast-falling lip-muted silver like a southern winter moonrise, 16-millimetre fisheye view, exploded vision, bubbles of froth bouncing back inside, liquid planes channelling the sight to a figure encapsulated under that lip coming down and along it, body bent tube crouch, left hand extended as if pointing a way.

A drawing left-hand beachbreak, a singular act beyond repetition, with a figure coming down its face, out from under a lip, racing both gravity and a surfing life's accumulated knowledge of consequences. A sequence of still frames follows. A drop, a turn, a climb, racing a wall, disappearance. The viewpoints are as total as the experience itself and are often established in the backrooms of 2 a.m.

Launching out to what? As a surfer I would have said it was obvious, but you still get asked often enough, because a lot of people sense correctly that it's just the tip of an iceberg.

SEA DREAMS

Sounds thundering in the night like a lost and landlocked surfer's dream. The stars splashed across the night sky, gleaming beacons, each one a long-lost friend, furrows in the sea of my past, but sweeping into the future with a thread of consistency.

Sirius, Canopus, Archenar ... a line taken from there to intersect another one here, and south is just across that hill, over there, where the sounds of Bass Strait are roaring and gnashing in the night.

It's been like this for three days straight, nearly eight foot. I was asked once, 'What do you do down here?' Well, what does any surfer do? It's only in ports and during flat stretches that the dream goes to bits, in hotels and cafes, drinking lattes and overhearing conversations that run, 'Honey, it doesn't have to be this way you know.'

Those night roarings are a sweet seductress all right, like shadows of sound, mutton-birds fluttering the water with their wings, primeval rhythms telling you clearly that you'll never quite leave your past, the places you've seen, the drops you've had, the sections you've made.

When roadsong breaks its cadence and the sounds of the sea take over, the stories of the night press forward to the fire's edge, fleshing out a surfing life. What's left to say after all this time? Perhaps only a tired voice, still defiant, but caught somewhere on the fringes of self pity ...

I'll never forget years later when I saw the book she'd written. I just couldn't believe it. At one stage I even considered using physical force with the publisher to stop it, but then decided against it.

The book was one of those coffee-table-type things. When I'd seen it I said to her, 'But we had an agreement to do it together. In that railway cutting north of Cairns we made a pact that we'd do it together.'

All she said was something like, 'Well it didn't come out that way. There's no need to be so neurotic about it.'

Everything was in the book. Absolutely everything. Our incredible flight from people, the police, from life itself. There were maps of the routes we'd taken, even place names were given, and at the back she'd put in one of those lists that tied up what had happened to all the characters in the book, neat biographical sketches on how everyone had finished up with the passing of time.

Well, I was in there all right, under another name. It mentioned something about Philippine faith healers. It also said that most of us were living in Carlton, which wasn't true. I'd never lived there. I was contemptuous of the place. I'd left the city in the mid '60s, and at the time this thing came out I was living on the coast surfing.

Roadsong is always a revelation.

EMIGRATION OF THE SPIRIT

Perfect waves at the end of roadsong? Is that how it goes? A strange blue sea, horizon straight, and those lumps forever passing by the eye's fevered disbelief. Sun-shafted rays reaching down to the water. Patterns from other places. Two female figures, one of them my wife, the other I don't know. Honey pots in the foreground, ambrosia perhaps. Weird vegetation and a confused, strange, half-Chinese sage out there like us all, just waiting, always waiting.

Animals moving about the foreshore in a manner suggesting they are the foreshore. Lizards. Scattered yellow banksia pods. Surfers rising and falling to an ever-constant swell.

Beyond the break line, at anchor, a cutter. What lands and swells and daemon winds has it felt? Voyages and fear-haunted nights on the seaway, beyond the coast and the reach of land. Ocean adventurer is not a term I would use.

An emigration of the spirit? Is that what it means? Like a gannet coming in low from the south, down the Winkipop swell line, its wingtips hanging just inches from the water, way out there. I have thought it means freedom, like roadsong itself, making your own way, with your own preconceived baggage, from the backrooms to the beach . . . to the where? What?

Under the Awnings

It was mid December and the wet season was still in the making. In some ways I always thought of it as the worst time of the year up there. Hot, humid, but still with a corner to turn. I never really got used to it. That evening, on the hill above the headland, the moist air hung heavily about us as we sat under the awnings on Melrose's verandah, desperate for the faintest wafts that struggled up from the sea below us.

From behind the point I could see the heaped whites and greys of the heavy rain clouds. Below us was a beach, and beyond it a reef that laid out from the point, shaping and moulding the final ramblings of a swell that was born hundreds of kilometres out to sea.

It was a dream of sorts, the type that hangs fleetingly at the edge of every surfing life. Tropical climate, warm waters, and relatively uncrowded good-quality waves. I guess a lot of people have picked up on it now in various ways, but back then, when this all happened, it was different and the paths were not nearly as well worn as they are now.

Melrose and I were having what I guess you'd call an indulgent conversation, a pot pourri of rambling analysis, poorly supported opinion, nostalgia and the hypothetical. We did it often enough, but never deluded ourselves as to the importance of what was said. That particular evening we were talking about surf dreams, pots of gold at the end of the rainbow, journeys along the old Silk Road, Samarkand, the outer reefs, and who knows where else.

It was Melrose's belief that the difficulty of the journey was what enhanced the destination. I think he even used the term 'pilgrim' and the phrase 'the sanctity of his vision'. I actually laughed at one stage but Melrose was serious.

'Look,' he said, reaching for a drink, 'I'll tell you a story and you see if what I've said doesn't mean something.'

I nodded and settled back as he brushed the droplets of iced water from his lips. He stood up and drew out a chart from the pile beside the window, opened it on the table in front of us, and then sat down.

'There are reefs here that have never been surfed.' And he laid his fingers on the chart to indicate the middle reaches of the Coral Sea to the west of Vanuatu. The dream was there all right, amid a mass of soundings, magnetic variations, tidal flows and datum heights.

'Quite a few years ago,' Melrose continued, 'I set sail from down south for those reefs with a guy named Bob Herrick, in his steel cutter *Southern Wave*. Herrick had some strange sides to him, and not everybody liked him. Maybe I understood him better than most. I'd grown up with him and we'd stayed in touch over the years, which was pretty remarkable given the way he did things.

'He was the type of person who'd just disappear from the scene for lengthy periods and no one would know where he'd got to. And then he'd just re-appear with these stories about poisonous snakes and church services in the Appalachian Mountains, that sort of stuff. Somebody said once he'd been reborn in Hawaii. Not everybody could take it. But that's just the way he was.

'I guess you'd call him a maritime wanderer. He'd done a lot of surfing throughout the Pacific in the days before surf camps and charter boats and all that bullshit, when you got yourself out there under your own devices, took what came and made of it what you wanted. Never a word of it got into a surf magazine either; that certainly wasn't his style.

'This time we were going via Lord Howe first, then north to those reefs. We'd planned to come back down the Queensland coast and hole up for the cyclone season in Mooloolaba.

'Right from the start we had gale-force headwinds and it wasn't too much of a trip. We couldn't lay our course and we were both sick as dogs. At one stage we discussed turning around and running back, but somehow held on and punched out further and further into the Tasman Sea. There were no GPS systems in those days and neither of us had a clue where we were.

'After four days of this, with no let up, we dropped sail and lay under bare poles for eighteen hours until it quietened down.

Actually, by that stage we were finding our sea-legs and becoming a pretty good team together. How long it would have lasted I'll never know, for just after we rehoisted sail again the main halyard broke and the whole trip kind of slid out of my hands.

'Herrick was an impetuous bastard. We should have waited for the sea to come down. At that stage the wind was easing and it was only a matter of time before the swell and chop fell away. We could have pushed on for a time with just the jib, and maybe even used the topping lift as a halyard. But he'd have none of it and rigged up the bosun's chair to be hoisted to the masthead to re-reeve a new mainsail halyard.

'We had no sail up and the yacht was rolling like blue blazes, the mast doing something like 90 degree arcs across the sky. I think he was about three-quarters of the way up when it happened. Either his grip slipped, or the crosstree fouled him, or something. Whatever it was he slipped out from under the rope supports of the bosun's chair, clutching for the mast. As the boat rolled he was flung, catapulted sideways, his chin hitting the crosstrees.

'From below the fall had the dimensions of a slow-motion nightmare. I watched as he fell six metres or so to the deck, his head striking it with the same dull sound of a pumpkin hitting concrete.

'Initially there was hardly a mark on him, but he was absolutely lifeless and blood was seeping from both his ears. Somehow I got him below and into a bunk, still unconscious. His pulse was reasonably strong and a time later the bleeding stopped. I'm no medical expert but I knew enough of the symptoms to figure serious internal injuries and that he needed pretty urgent attention.

'Resetting the jib, I brought the yacht around and ran off with the wind and waves in the general direction of the coast. For a time I sat at the tiller and laid out logically in my mind the things to be done. I knew I could establish our position later that day if the sun got out from behind the clouds, and from there determine a course to a settlement with medical facilities. We had no radio transmitter, just a receiver, and I knew it would be at least another forty-eight hours before we got near the shipping lanes.

'Using the topping lift I reset the mainsail, and as the weather eased later in the morning shook out the reefs and went below to the chart table to prepare for some attempt at estimating our position. I had just finished marking up a dead-reckoning position when a movement caused me to look up to the side. I was staring straight down the barrel of a rifle and above it were Herrick's unsteady eyes.

'His face was a sickly white, misshapen from the swelling which was setting in, and the eyes were misaligned and out of plumb. For a moment when he first spoke to me I thought he might have been delirious. But the broken phrases and the paranoia quickly made it obvious that it was something far worse than that. The fall had obviously precipitated some sort of mental collapse. He was totally unbalanced.

'At first I tried to reason with him, but it was no good. He had some fixation about my taking his boat and dumping him overboard. He forced me up on deck and made me sit on the cabin top just aft of the mast. For a time I logically argued with him, but it was useless. He either disregarded my explanations or parried them with more illogical accusations. At one point I attempted to approach him, only to be halted as the rifle was levelled at me.

'Late in the afternoon he ordered all the sail dropped and we lay wallowing in the swells. Then began the second stage of this madness, the Bible quotes, and predictions of a great storm in which all the sinners would perish. I can now scarcely remember the complete rantings of that afternoon because they all just started to run together.

'At one stage he came out with a garbled version of Psalm 24, and I can distinctly remember the sinister, almost theatrical tone of his voice as he finished: "For he hath finished it upon the seas. And established it upon the floods."

'By dusk I was close to exhaustion, but Herrick seemed unaltered. Maybe you've seen booze and drugs alter people you thought you knew pretty well, so that reason no longer can touch them. You can be an inch from their faces and still not be able to get to them. Well, it was like that only a hundred times worse. He wasn't ever going to sober up.

'Periodically the outbursts would come, his face contorting in anger. And then he lapsed into a brooding silence. For a moment I thought that perhaps he'd come out of it, but just as dark was coming on he ordered the dinghy to be cut loose from the cabin top and launched.

'As I struggled to do this he regaled me with an account of the storm which would soon engulf the yacht and the retribution which would befall the sinners on board.

'When the dinghy was launched he came forward from the cockpit, swung his legs over the lifelines and deftly stepped down onto the centre thwart. In a moment he'd cast off and was adrift at the stern, a pathetic figure grappling with the oars.

'For some moments I sat watching him row, disappearing from time to time in the troughs. God knows where he thought he was headed. Then I started the engine and made the first of three attempts to recover him. But each time I came up on him the rifle rose up threateningly and on the second run he shattered the timber rail of the cockpit coaming with a shot.

'After that I hung off, hoping that in the darkness I could surprise him. Then I made one last attempt. I had the boathook ready to knock the rifle aside and drag him on board. For one second I thought it would work, but at the last moment the dinghy rolled and I missed him. As I slid past he swore at me and tried to level off for another shot. I left him astern and sat down to think.

'It seemed hopeless. By morning I figured he could be dead from a brain haemorrhage, and besides, I'd never figured myself as a hero.

'I threw the gear lever into forward and came back on course for the coast. Astern in the moonlight I could see the dinghy rising and falling, a small figure bent to the oars. And then it disappeared, and all that remained was the phosphorescence of the wake and the terrible truth of the open ocean.'

Melrose finished and reached out to refill his empty glass. For some time I didn't speak except to mutter 'phew' or some equally mundane expression.

'Oh, it's true all right,' Melrose eventually said, 'just as true as I stand here. I had God's own trouble with the authorities when I got in four days later. No one would believe me.' For a moment he was silent, and then he said, 'I still haven't surfed those reefs, but when I do I'll have made the pilgrim's journey a hundred times over.'

Tube Ride

A coarse-sanded beach of yellow–black headlands and half-moon caves, washed by an evening's purple winter moonrise. Light fading. Footprints in the clay had come together to make a twisted trail that cut down an erosion gully to a narrow concourse. Someone had edged in steps and later the sleepers had been put down. A surfer's path. Across to the right was a rough-hewn outcrop of sandstone, its base littered with broken boulders. Out to sea ran a long shelving rock ledge, down which the swell would roll.

That day I'd been surfing with him; in fact, we'd gone out together. But I'd come in early and now I was just watching from the clifftop, cocooned in that winter weather surfer's afterglow. His wife was there too, and we stood side by side talking. After all the time they'd been together I could never work out why she still sometimes came out with him. She often said things about him that disturbed me and left me wondering what was the amalgam of their relationship.

'Isn't it time we had a little honesty about all this?' she said to me that evening in a flat almost vacuous voice, her gaze going straight past me and out over the water. 'You're one of his friends. Did you know he was photographed by the police one time?'

I said I didn't.

'Well, he was,' she said. 'It was on the Yarra bank sometime around the first anti-Vietnam demos. I think they were trying to intimidate him. In those days, as you well know, it didn't take much for them to open a file on you, and life could become very difficult. I don't think he ever really got over it. Paranoia can be very easily seeded.'

As she spoke, across the car park a radio was playing the Chuck Berry tune 'Promised Land'. That's where we were all right.

Out to sea a set had appeared, the wavefaces a deep plum colour, drawing with that other-world smoothness you sometimes see just on dusk. He'd moved in deeper than the others. When I'd been out in the water with him I'd seen him do it a hundred times. The distant dark intimation of an approaching set, most of us scrambling to get out and across. Then a glance inside to see him stroking 'over there', always with that shoulder-dip paddle, a dig-in-deep-hunched-up action that gave him a lean and hungry look. Which he was, because there was no denying it, he was a killer out there.

His boards were always a celebration and it never really mattered to me whether or not he ever caught a wave on them.

Some had Sanskrit figures on them, which left you wondering where they'd been. Another time the boards would all be a liturgical Lenten soft-wash purple, or just black all over. This one was a five-foot-nine twin fin, and it should have been hanging in a public gallery somewhere. I remember he rode it that big Easter Saturday morning. 'An exploration of the limits,' he called it, then smilingly added, 'I think I found them . . . for this board, at least!'

I suppose 'creative' is the best word to describe not only his boards, but the whole way he went about surfing. There was one Saturday afternoon I remember where he surfed his way back along the coast to Torquay from Southside by picking up waves here and there, paddling a few hundred metres then another ride and so on. I guess you'd call it cross-country surfing. Not many people do it, but that's how he was, so nothing he did ever really surprised me.

In the evening light he went into the tube from a long way back. The angle seemed all wrong. I mean, I knew that from where we were on the clifftop. There was just nowhere to go . . . or . . . well, apparently there *was* because he never made any real drop. Somehow he turned at almost the same instant as his feet hit the deck. A fantastic arching movement that took the board's trajectory from one plane to another, almost irrespective of the waveface, the push, the gravity and a hundred other physical laws screaming their logic in the back of my mind.

And then he was gone, our view of him taken by the foam-flecked falling wall behind which his figure moved along, locked into an almost martial stance, rigid yet infinitely flexible, responding to a million intricate stimuli and data crying out for physical and cerebral analysis, almost before conscious registration. An angle at the foot, shivers and vibrations coming from the soles of the feet, or the knees, or a vision ahead impressing itself with a swimmingly strange enclosure and those other-world sounds; all forward movement seemingly stopped, he told me later, like the centre of a turning world rushing past him.

One time off Rincon I'd seen him in 'there' from the water, as I clawed my way up a waveface and looked back down along its corkscrewing face and loud hissing twist to where he was slotted in. All the way and speeding, that was the flash. One of those things you get almost every time you surf if you keep your eyes open. One of those if-I-had-a-camera type things that are all the better for not having a camera, just a light-sensitive mind making its own indelible images.

Well, this was the same. He never made it out, but from the point he entered until we saw his board come up out of the foam, and then his head, was time and distance enough for me and then some. It was fantastic. Three of us had seen it. Just three. His wife who had probably seen it all before, myself, and the Chuck Berry song car owner.

I felt I had to say something, because I didn't think anybody else was going to. I remembered how he had always been suspicious of media attention and the whole process by which something as simple as a tube ride could appear in the magazines and be turned into something else altogether. With that thought in my mind I fumbled for the right words. 'When you see things like that,' I said, 'you have to ask yourself where exactly in all this does the glare have to fit?'

For the first time in our conversation his wife looked at me. I think she knew what I was getting at. 'It doesn't. It just doesn't have any place at all,' she said, 'it's not even a small part of the bigger picture.'

I knew exactly what she meant, because I've always had trouble with the glare. In fact, over the years I've spent a lot of time wondering about it, not just in surfing, but in other things too. It was fairly early in the piece when I was first told, but almost from the day I heard that my rock idol Tommy filled out the front of his trousers with newspaper I've wondered about the glare. 'It never fails to get a scream,' he'd said.

And of course at a later stage there were those fantastic tours he did. Empty yellow eyeballs and no one at home behind them. An act that went on stage playing fifteen-year-old hits he'd written, followed up by a monotone voice asking the audience what they wanted to hear, and then giving it to them with weird lapses, such as when the band opened with one number and he started to sing another.

Someone said he was 'not entirely conversant with the numbers being played', but we all knew that. The promoters cut the tour short after just three one-night stands on the Melbourne suburbs' pub circuit. People were trying to get at Tommy from the audience to punch him out. Ever since then I've wondered about the glare and what it does to people. In the end you're left asking just how much icing does the cake have to have?

So there we were that evening on the clifftop, in the fading light watching the tube ride. When it was over and he came in I thought I heard him use a term — 'the rush' — or something like it.

His wife told me, some time after this, on another clifftop, that in her opinion most surfers were 'fucking neurotics'.

The Storm

He had been alone at sea for three days. In the beginning there had been calms and long oily swells that had rolled in from the south and reminded him of his surfing. For almost his entire life ocean swells had been a constant for him, underscoring in part how and where he lived. Sometimes he rode them, at other times he swam or dived in them, or sailed across them. Sometimes they frightened the hell out of him. At other times they made him seasick and for the first day of this trip he had felt unwell, his heart only half in it. Surfing was always much easier, he had mused at the time.

On the third afternoon he made his landfall on the southeastern coast, and with it there came the excitement that always came as a cloud lifted, and a hill or mountain took shape on the horizon where he had hoped it would. This time it had been part of the east coast alps, and the man had gone below to make note of the landfall in his logbook.

Just as he finished the entry he flicked the switch of the small transceiver beside his chart table and heard the first of the storm warnings. The voice was as impartial as ever: '. . . a depression of . . . hectopascals, centred . . . moving eastwards at . . .' The man listened as the voice monotonously sounded its warnings. '. . . winds of 60 knots with higher squalls over an area bounded by . . . decreasing to 40 knots . . .' A quick check confirmed that the depression would sweep by just to the south of him later that same day. As the warnings finished the man tapped the barometer mounted on the bulkhead next to him. It fell several points.

Emerging from the cabin he stood in the cockpit, bracing himself against the motion of the boat. Ahead he could now clearly see the mountains and coastline taking shape. The sky was cloudy and in spite of an indirect sun it was strangely humid and warm. A sizeable swell was making in from the southeast, generated by the storm he had just heard of. To the south he could discern the tops of anvil-shaped clouds that lay heavily merged with the horizon.

If the forecast was correct then he had some hours before the winds would progressively strengthen and in that time it would be important that he get as far away as possible from the land. What had been a blessing was now a concern. Releasing the tiller lashings of his self-steering mechanism, the man swung the yacht about, re-trimmed the sails for a new heading and set out diagonally from the coast on a northeasterly heading.

Now was the time to firmly stow all the loose gear, and as the yacht pranced across the swells the man went forward to check the lashings which held the dinghy to the cabin top. Satisfied, he came back to the cabin, compensating almost automatically for the yacht's movements as he did so. Below, he wedged his navigation books into their shelves, checked that the food cupboards were secure, then set about preparing a meal for himself. It would be important that he eat now, for there would be no telling what conditions would arise later.

When he had finished the food and come out from the cabin, he noticed that the wind had strengthened markedly and was blowing from the southeast. He didn't like it at all and his unease pressed uncomfortably on his chest. For a moment his mind sought a refuge in some unrelated subject. With this swell and wind any number of South Coast surf breaks would be working, he mused and a list of names rolled across his thoughts then passed just as quickly, driven on by the inevitability of his present.

Behind him, far out in the wake, the land was only a smudge on the horizon, blending and merging with the lower-lying clouds. In the southwest, and now extending across the horizon, he could plainly see the storm clouds heaped up in a roll of grey that ran in a broad sweep along the line of his vision. Where they met the sea in the far distance the man could see a greyish-green light, which caught the vivid white tops of the wavelets that had formed atop the swells. When those clouds rolled over him, he knew the wind would probably veer to the southwest and the real business of this storm would begin.

By now the yacht was leaping and racing forward, its lee gunwale held firmly at water level. As it thrust through the waves, water would race down the tilted deck, striking the cleats and winch mountings, throwing up geysers of spray which fell on the cabin roof or into the cockpit. If he was to be free from the fear of being blown onto the coast, then he knew that every sea mile made good now would be insurance for the time when it might be impossible to sail.

An hour later the decision on how long he might go on for was made for him, as the wind speed increased and the boat began to lurch heavily from the press of sail. Crabbing his way from handhold to handhold he crawled to the mast and set about reefing the mainsail to reduce its area. After that he dropped the headsail and set the storm jib in its place. He'd done both these things enough times now for them to be routine physical procedures. But each time still carried its own unique uncertainties, a half-defined dread he assumed might stay with him always, in much the same way that he still asked himself, 'What will happen today?' whenever he paddled out into big surf.

When he finished the sail changes and looked astern he could no longer see the land. Instead the sea and clouds were fusing in a sickly dark grey. The sun had been overpowered and was now completely hidden behind the huge roll of cloud that dominated three-quarters of the sky. At the front of the cloud bolts of lightning were arcing down to the water in places. An eerie almost unreal light seemed to come from all directions and the vividness of the white caps on top of the swells was even more marked than earlier.

For a time the man stood watching, drawn by some horrid fascination at the preface to his ordeal. He had never seen such heavy clouds, nor such a sudden preamble. As he turned his back to it to study the yacht's behaviour, he tried to draw comfort from the hope that such a sudden build-up might foretell only a short sudden storm. But he wasn't sure and his uneasiness increased. For the moment there was nothing much more he could do, but sit in the cockpit with the cold dryness in his mouth and the tightness in his stomach, watching the scene unfold.

As the day's light was lost and the storm front moved in above him, the southeast wind momentarily faltered and puffs of cold air mixed with its lukewarm remnants. Then it just died and heavy droplets of rain began to fall. About him, lightning was crackling down and it seemed that a cloak of blackness was being flung across the sea. At the same instant, the wind veered to the southwest and hit him with an unbelievable ferocity.

Clutching a torch he struggled forward to the mast and lowered the mainsail. As he lay over the boom, gathering it in on itself, it flogged against his face. With a length of line he lashed it down and wrapping his arms around the mast peered into the darkness. He could see very little and was really only aware of noise and terrible sounds. All about him the wind pressed against his clothing, tearing at his hair and setting up a vile high-pitched scream in the rigging above him.

The yacht was now reaching across the wind and seas with only one sail set. The self-steering gear was having trouble handling the pressures generated by the wind strength. The man made some adjustments to its setting and retired below. He lay in the darkness trying to gauge the yacht's behaviour. In spite of his activities he was not yet tired. As he lay on the bunk, wedged by cushions against the boat's motion, he was surprised at the clarity with which he was thinking. He tried to account for each creak, every hiss and slap. It amazed him how much he and the yacht had merged. It was as if they had been flung together into a melting pot and would be fused together for the length of the ordeal. A short time later he realised that to continue with even one sail set was foolish.

In the blackness on the deck he was greeted by a scene of utter confusion. Around him he was aware of terrible, almost primordial movements, as huge black shapes hissed past the boat. He could hear them thundering in the distance and as the noise grew louder he would hold on and wait. They would roar up like approaching trains, sometimes breaking 'out there' across from him, or just behind him. He was thankful that it was night and he couldn't see them.

Above him the wind was now shrieking in the rigging. It was unlike anything he had ever heard. As he lay pressed to the deck and inching forward he wondered at the velocity which could set up such a wail. He supposed the gusts might be Force 10, and for a moment odd phrases of description from the Beaufort Scale came to him '. . . very high waves, long overhanging crests . . . tumbling seas, dense white streaks'.

As he knelt on the foredeck, clawing at the flogging sail above him, he felt the deck sink below him and instinctively clasped for a handhold. A moment later the first wave broke clean across the deck, washing up to his armpits. In a frenzy he dragged the jib to the deck and tied it to the metal railings of the pulpit. Trembling with cold he scuttled hand-over-hand to the cockpit. For a moment he sat, overcome by the movement and noise about him.

Even without a stitch of sail the yacht was moving quite fast with the wind and occasionally a steeper wave would lift it up and thrust it forward, slithering down the waveface in a smother of foam. Even in his dazed state he realised that one of these surges would eventually lead to the yacht broaching and being rolled down by the following sea. Reaching into the locker beside his feet, he uncoiled a nylon anchor warp and after securing one end to a cleat on the aft deck began paying out the remainder of the line. As the drag came on, the effect was noticeable and the yacht's speed slowed, and its tendency to shoot was reduced. It was also his last defensive measure, and after relashing the tiller he retired below, knowing that he had done everything that he could to save himself and the yacht.

If conditions worsened he would be powerless. Yet strangely he felt almost elated. As the feeling ran through him he lowered himself onto the cabin floor, and still in his wet weather gear lay huddled below the chart table. Quite suddenly a great lethargy fell over him. He looked at his watch — it was just after midnight. The storm was five hours old.

In the darkness that followed, the man lay braced across the cabin floor. Despite his tiredness, sleep refused to come and he found himself wondering as to the strength of his rigging, the rudderpost and even the hull itself. For the first time now the boat was being forcibly struck by broken waves. As he lay with his ear to the floor he could sense what was happening outside by the angle of incline, and sometimes the rumbling of an approaching roller came in above the whine of the wind. When they crashed against the hull the noise would reverberate around him as a sickening thud and the yacht would lay over before righting itself with water streaming from its cabin top and decks. Even with no sail set, it now lay for most of the time at a heel of forty degrees and the interval between the breaking waves was becoming shorter.

With his head cradled on his arms he lay listening. He felt utterly powerless and half wished something might happen to give him something to do. Then he took his sleeping bag, and wrapping it around his head attempted to obliterate the terrible noises from outside. For a while he was aware only of the sharp pitching and rearing of the boat around him. He thought about praying but couldn't. It somehow seemed inappropriate, however scared he was.

Then, in one moment of clarity it suddenly came to him what the term 'founder' meant. It had two senses, and now in the darkness he had finally and truthfully come across the seaman's sense of the word. It meant to be totally overwhelmed. He supposed that if he never made it back to the coast then somewhere they would say that he had 'foundered'. It was a revelation for him.

At almost the same moment it came to him, he heard a terrible noise that came through the sleeping bag pressed against his ears. As he sat up he sensed rather than saw the angle on which the yacht lay. It was a jerking movement and it thrust him against the side of the hull. The full enormity hit him when he realised that the floor on which he had been lying was for a moment vertical beside him. The yacht had been knocked down.

In a welter of falling objects, the man reached out to wedge himself. For an instant the yacht lay on its side and then slowly shook itself free, and with water cascading from its deck, began to right itself. It was then that the second wave hit. From inside the cabin the man knew something serious had happened, for the tremble that ran through the hull at the moment of impact seemed to come from the keel. At the same instant, water shot into the cabin and from outside came a tearing sound, harsh, above the wind. It was the dinghy. Torn from its lashings above the cabin it had been swept overboard. Below where it had been, the cabin roof and two side windows were breached. As successive smaller waves rolled across the yacht it slowly began to fill.

It took the man a moment to stumble over the debris and locate the damage. By the time he did so water was above the floorboards, pitching against the hull every time the yacht rolled. With the added weight inside it, the yacht's motion was becoming sluggish and the man realised that if it continued to rise he would lose any reserve buoyancy, and with it his life.

Clutching a bundle of soaked blankets, bunk cushions and his sleeping bag, he jammed them into the splintered holes of the cabin sides. It wasn't enough to stop the flow that continued every time a wave washed over, but perhaps it would win him the time to at least get through the worst.

Slumping aft, he cleared the squat handle of the bilge pump and began to move it, backwards and forwards. The motion was a short sharp push and pull, and as the man began to feel the water press on the pump diaphragm he braced himself against the pitching hull by holding onto the galley bench. Surging around his feet in the water was a vile slop of softened fruit, wet newspaper, clothing and broken food packets. Sometimes it fouled the strainer of the pump and he would stop to locate the end of the hose and clear it away.

After a time he changed hands, but the water still washed around him. As his arm tired he changed again. The pace of his pumping slowed and the length of time between changes shortened. Still the water washed at his feet and the terrible roar outside continued. He didn't know if he was making progress. All he knew was that the surge about him continued.

He tried to visualise what state the sea outside might be in. He did it only to forget the aching in his arms, and he supposed that by now the tops of the waves were being scooped off by the wind, and white foam would lie scattered across the sea.

By now he was oblivious to the yacht's movements. As he pumped and cleared and cleared and pumped, he tried different positions, but always one arm, then the other. He tried not to look at the water level, hoping that when he next did it might have noticeably dropped. He counted the strokes, then took turn about, one hundred for each arm. As time passed he lowered it, sixty for each arm. Then he tried a spell with both arms together.

In time the noise outside had become a dull roar. The man could hear another noise, welded to the laboured, heavy panting of his breath. This noise came from within his head. He watched his hands and tried to divorce them from his body. He willed them to continue. He promised them a break if they did fifteen more strokes, then another fifteen, and then another fifteen.

Vague flashes of light passed before his eyes, whites and reds. His breath felt like fire. Exhaustedly, he paused. From deep inside him came a terrific wave. He lifted his head and vomited onto the floor as the wave engulfed him. Then he fell. As his head lay on the floorboards he was aware of a wet wood smell. But no water washed his face. It was below the floorboards.

When he awoke it was light and the wind, while still fresh, had fallen. Around him mountainous seas of grey reared and pitched. They were terrible, but without the spur of the strongest winds they would in time fall. As he stared at the boat from the cockpit, at its partly splintered cabin top, at the frayed ends of the dinghy lashings and the torn and shredded jib still tied to the pulpit railings, he began to laugh. From deep inside, with a hungered stomach, he laughed that he was still alive. Surfing might drown you, he thought, but this was something else.

The Low Road to Xanadu

In the early summer we took the low road, with the hills still spread under the growths of spring. Flashes of colour fell across our path — azures, yellows, the mottled barks of tall, tall trees and the stumpy brown-fronded verdants of ageless ferns. Gullies encrusted with rich growths of moss, vine and creeper, spilling down hillsides to the lush pastures edged with fable, myth and allegory.

The low road to Xanadu laid out in a sweep through rounded hills, descending to the flat expanses of a coast caught midway between fast-eroding bluffs, and an ever-pounding, lifefull sea. The low road, shimmering in its southern light, laid down like a strip of black licorice, snaking its way west.

At one time we came out from the hills and touched the coast in the night, and they were there, there in the black, in silver-dappled lines, moving, moving, the peaks peeling off with an almost ectoplasmic whiteness, illuminated and illuminating as if lit by car headlights from above and below.

Visions came to us with an increasing rapidity. Winter and the first fickle touches of a northerly zephyr over the dune tops. Offshore yellow dunes and green-washed coastal grasses. Headlands and beaches eroded and eaten, succumbing to the endless surge of storms, yielding their quotas of particle. Resistance here and there in the form of bleak solitary sculptured outcrops, disciples to the constancy of wind and wave, that tourists gaze out over, waiting for some magic to wash over them.

Ice-cold numbings breaking into the sweaty warmth of a wetsuit. Shock-breath-inducing cold washes that numb the head. Paddling to evermore at any one of a thousand spots. Visions of life or death or both, on primeval greybeards. I've wondered out there at times if ever I would return to the beach. Out there, cut off from the shore by a gulf, with the mind's doors beginning to open, with imagination paralysing rationality and beginning its explorations of the possibilities.

40°S. How easily it rolls off the tongue.

A place that hovers stoically on the edge of the world's great westerly belt. The Roaring Forties. Named for the noise that set up, down there, in a ship's rigging. That and the waves.

The Roaring Forties, an expressway for the clipper ships running the world round with scarcely a smattering of land to impede the wind's way, or the watery wastes of the Southern Ocean.

Patagonia and the Argentine coast, then nothing. Nothing but the wastes of an ocean so grey its loneliness haunted the sailors who scarred its surface, trailing their albatross and cold, cold memories. Not for them the milk of paradise.

> Fetch: the uninterrupted stretch of water over which the wind can operate. The longer the fetch the higher the waves.
>
> Frank Robb: *Handling Small Craft in Heavy Weather*

Patagonia and the Argentine coast, then nothing. Nothing. An uninterrupted stretch of water.

> Big waves, I thought, but how odd that Russians measured in feet. I looked closer. The wave heights were not in feet at all, they were in metres. Waves 105 ft high!
>
> David Lewis: *Icebird*.

Patagonia and the Argentine coast, then nothing. Nothing. An uninterrupted stretch of water.

> November 25 . . . that evening a big swell began running in suddenly from the west, big, I would say, 50ft.
>
> Francis Chichester: *Gypsy Moth Circles the World*.

An uninterrupted stretch of water, and along its northern edge, the west wind and the deep, deep depressions are fielded and bounded by a coast that stretches from Cape Leeuwin west to Cape Otway and south to the Maatsykers. Peripheral energies only, for the mass of it all passes below Tasmania, with just a residue rolling itself onto the west Tasmanian or King Island coasts, or jams itself through into Bass Strait to come ashore at the likes of Bells or Gunnamatta.

> Monster waves shown to be real ... German scientists have explained the mystery behind so-called monster waves — the term given by oceanographers for near vertical breaking seas up to 40 metres high.
>
> *The Age*

Whispering's of things unknown. Intimations hidden behind the unemotional officialese of Admiralty Chart 1695B. 40°40' S, 144°10'E — Bell Reef, just there suddenly coming up from the depths. 39°34'S 143°56'E — Harbinger Reef, with the annotation next to it on the chart: 'Always breaks.' A host of others. Waterwitch Reef. Black Pyramid. There is no land to the west for 6000 miles. In the bleak black nights of winter, what energy dissipates itself down there, I wonder? What shapes are thrown and walls set up, never to be ridden? Power pockets of another dimension?

Ah, Xanadu ... something wonderful, powerful, basic, where waves can dredge up from off any of a myriad uncharted reefs.

> There were four waves in front of it, all over 15 ft, yet this one could be seen clearly above the rest ... It was the largest wave I have ever seen from the water. It was perfect, unbelievably clean and formed. How big? We couldn't say. It was beyond our comprehension.
>
> Wayne Lynch: *The Outer Reef*

Xanadu, where the moon can hang blood red in the black night sky, lighting the way and the truth, and the banshee wail of a winter sou'wester can thick the air with spume and salt spray. Where the tale told by the idiot, full of sound and fury, might sometimes just signify something and relight the brief candle.

In the early summer we took the low road to Xanadu. We were not the first that ever burst into that silent sea, for surfers have visited its shores for years. Changes have been made, and though it is no longer what it was, it is also not yet what it will become.

We took the low road to Xanadu, and though we did not die, we were all changed.

Tattoo

Dennis was grinning when he stood up from the tattoo table, but his face looked pale and strained. A piece of paper towelling had been taped to his biceps and Greeves could see a bloodstain spreading out from the centre of it.

'Your turn now, mate,' Dennis said as he moved to the pool table at the front of the shop. There was a studied remoteness about him that Greeves could never quite grasp. He always called you 'mate', but it really meant nothing. Even when they surfed together Dennis would say things like, 'You take this one, mate,' but drop in on him just the same. Over the years Dennis had taken so many of his waves that Greeves had lost count. That's just how it was.

Greeves looked up at the yellowing walls. Around him, on laminated cardboard, hung numbered examples of the tattooist's work. Dragons and fantasy scenes, bleeding hearts and motifs danced in a random wash of tattoo blues and reds, yellows, greens and blacks.

Greeves walked to the table. The tattooist's face looked as if it had been in a bad car accident. It was pushed in and oddly misshapen, with scars that ran across his forehead and the bridge of his nose. Greeves thought that at some stage he might have been a boxer.

The tattooist's name was Norman Master. On the window of the shop among a mass of technicolour designs was a printed board with the words 'The Master of Tattooists'. There was also a list of famous people with tattoos, like Sean Connery and Lady Randolph Churchill and a few others Greeves had never heard of.

'How old are you, son?' the tattooist asked. But before Greeves could reply he went on, 'Which one do you want?'

'Eighteen,' Greeves lied, and then, pointing at the wall above him, said 'That one there. Number twenty-seven.' It was a skull pierced from top to bottom by a stiletto and underneath a scroll captioned with the words 'Death Never Sleeps'.

'The last person I did that for was Ray Johnson, the welterweight,' the tattooist said. 'A fucking lot of good it did him. Lost his title the very next fight. That's forty bucks.' He waited for Greeves to get out the notes, twenty and two tens, then flicked through a sheaf of tissue stencils that lay in an expandable file at his feet.

As he did so Greeves saw the continuous blue patterning that reached down his arms, ending with an amateurishly drawn set of chain bracelets encircling each wrist.

Suddenly Greeves hoped his arms would never finish up looking like that. One didn't make much difference. That was

Dennis's idea. But whatever happened he didn't want to end up with arms like that. They just looked shithouse. It was just as his mother kept trying to tell him. 'Things don't have to be that way,' she'd say, but he never knew what she really meant. It was easier to drift along and go surfing with Dennis and let him call you 'mate'.

'Where do you want it?' the tattooist asked. Greeves indicated a spot, his left arm cocked across the table like a broken wing. He could see the bottles, the needles, the caps of brightly coloured inks, the sprays and antiseptic and paper towel. The tattoo gun lay on its side, its wires reaching up into the darkness next to the low-hanging fluorescent light.

The tattooist dabbed at his arm with a shaving brush he'd drawn up from a discoloured mug of lukewarm soapy water. He then reached for a razor.

Greeves allowed his eyes to move up the wall behind the tattooist, past the spread legs of the pin-ups, to a sign that refused service to minors and drunks and persons with venereal disease. If only Walsh could see me now, Greeves thought.

Walsh had been one of Greeves's teachers at the local school, one of the ones who always played for the laughs. 'Greeves,' he would say, 'you're blessed with the gift of eternal youth, in the form of permanently arrested mental development.' Or sometimes, 'Greeves, if you had another brain it'd be lonely.'

In the laughter that inevitably followed Greeves would silently squirm and smoulder. One day Dennis winked at him when the others were laughing, and Greeves felt better about things, although he didn't know why.

Walsh's wife was also a teacher and every year they went to Europe for their holidays.

One day Greeves pinned a used condom he'd found behind the science block to Walsh's staffroom door. He was never caught, and later he overheard Walsh ranting about the 'animals' he had to teach and how he'd get out of it all if it wasn't for his superannuation. It made Greeves feel good just to hear it. Walsh had his suspicions, but he could never pin them down. 'Greeves, you'll come to a sticky end,' he said one day.

The stencil left the pattern clearly outlined on his skin and Greeves watched as the tattooist lifted the gun, inserted a needle, dipped its tip into a cap of black ink and leaned forward to etch in the outline. A finely pitched zinging cut the air.

At first it felt like a tickle, or some reasonably minor skin irritation. Greeves wondered what all the fuss was about. 'They don't exactly tickle,' someone had once said to him.

Zing . . . dab . . . zing, zing, zing . . . dab, dab . . . zing, zing, zing, zing.

The line was making steady progress and the tattooist stopped periodically to dab and check his line. Blood had begun to seep out in small droplets and these were mixing with the black ink that lay smeared across his arm. The tattooist would stop to sponge them away using a half sponge that lay in an enamel bowl beside him.

By now Greeves's arm was beginning to throb and the area of the tattoo was burning. He was glad when the needle was changed and a new colour field begun. The colours were vivid, especially the blacks, but the whole thing was puffy looking, raised and inflamed, and the tattooist was continually sponging at the blood and dyes.

'You feeling all right?' the tattooist asked. Greeves nodded, but his head felt light. 'There's no stopping now, son,' the tattooist said. 'You got no choice.'

Greeves let his eyes wander back to the pin-ups. Choice. He remembered Dennis saying to him the night Sharon James had knocked him back in the sand hills behind the surf beach, 'You don't give her any choice, mate, either she does it or she walks home.'

That same night had been the first time Greeves had beaten Dennis at pool. They'd started on fifty-cent games, and Greeves had won the first when Dennis put the black down. He hadn't liked it and kept pressing for a return at double-or-quits. Greeves had taken him again and again, then again. By eight-thirty that night Dennis owed him thirty-two dollars, but Greeves knew he'd never collect. It would go on until he lost. Even so, he knew that some kind of balance had been tipped. It was only a small thing and it was just a feeling he had.

'That's it,' the tattooist said. Suddenly the zinging stopped and the tattoo was done. It lay there on his arm. Greeves looked at the brilliant hues, reds and yellows and blacks, so clear and alive that he hoped they wouldn't have to be covered with paper and that they would last like that forever.

Then the blood started to seep out again and the edge was lost. The tattooist gave it one final wipe, then smoothed petroleum jelly across the whole area. Somehow the shininess of it intensified the colours and the tattoo fairly leapt to life.

The tattooist placed a length of paper across Greeves's arm and taped it with two lines of sticky tape. He gave Greeves a card. On one side it read *Norman Master: The Master of Tattooists* and on the other was a list of do's and don'ts in caring for the tattoo. It listed things like avoiding sunburn and not picking at the scabs.

Greeves joined Dennis at the front of the shop. Nothing was said.

They pushed through the plastic fly strips of the doorway out into the noise of the street, their arms conspicuously papered just below the sleeves of their T-shirts.

Suddenly Dennis tore the paper away from his own arm. 'None of this shit for me, mate,' he said, and threw the paper onto the pavement.

Greeves wished Dennis had said 'us' and not just 'me'. As the thought came to him he suddenly knew something else, with a certainty he had never known before about anything.

The tattoo didn't alter a thing. It made no difference. He was on his way . . . and it was all for nothing. He was finished with Dennis and from now on he would surf by himself.

Wind on the Water

REFLECTIONS

The swell had been weak for almost all of that year. People were talking about fundamental shifts in the earth's weather systems. The papers and the talkback radio shows had latched on to the floods in January, the snows in February, the March heatwaves and other extraordinary empiricals as some sort of evidence that things were out of kilter. There was mention that the weather had 'gone mad', but it never seriously worried me. I was happy enough to take it as it came, and I knew it would come. It always does. If not tomorrow, then certainly the day after.

On the beach the sand swept through a semicircle, the tips of which ended in the ochre-and-dun-coloured cliffs of sparsely vegetated headlands. Off both of them a swell was breaking, peeling down a half-tide rock shelf in a desultory fashion. If you had asked me were there waves I would have said, 'Yes, but only if you're desperate.' It wasn't what I would call surf. But the signs were there. The wind was back in the northwest and swell-lines could be seen out at sea from the car park at the tip of the northern headland, faint and indistinct, almost like brushstrokes of wind on the water.

The movement of the swell itself was a stippling. I've seen flocks of mutton-birds create this same effect when you disturb them on a calm sea. The flutter of the wings, the movement of the feet centimetres above the surface, and the sound, creates a swirl of sensation, a noise and movement that sweeps across the water as the flock rises, then just as quickly fades and is lost. Well, this swell was something similar, patches of silent stippling coming forward, not in unbroken lines as it does when there is strength to it, but subtle and irregular, here and there. If you were surfing, there would have been long waits between waves.

The sand of the beach had a strange light to it. The sun was just up but a cloudbank masked it. The effect was a golden grey and the air had a restful feel to it, like a sigh during sex.

Down from the car park small groups of people had gathered and were carrying camera boxes and light reflectors onto the sand. It was some type of photo shoot. I nodded to one of the women in the group as I passed by. She was talking to the others and I heard her use the term 'the frontier of surfing'.

It was mid tide, and below the rubble of rock at the cliff base the beach sloped gently down to the water's edge. Every so often the surge of a wave would sweep up the sand, completely clearing it of markings and footprints, leaving a finely granulated surface, pristine and virginal.

As yet another wave performed this cleansing ritual a small fragment of something caught my eye. It had been deposited midway between the water and the rocks, and only stood out because of the smoothness of the sand.

At first I thought it was a pebble washed up or uncovered by the incessant movement of the water. Two or three steps from it I realised it was something else, a fragment of glass, no bigger than my thumbnail, silver–green with sea age and smooth beyond comprehension.

I knew at once where it had come from. Barely half a kilometre across the beach from where I stood, the torn and rusted remains of a clipper ship lay scattered along the length of the reef that skirted the headland. Over the years I had dived and explored and sought out its relics of door handles, glass and china fragments, slate and rust-fused metal. That's where this little piece had come from, after a journey of a hundred years. I picked it up and put it in my pocket, my fingers sliding across its irregular smooth surface. Wave energy, I mused.

Captain Chapman had made a solitary small mistake. One dark May night he mistook the lights of a coffee palace on the clifftops for a lighthouse, and the waves did the rest.

Close to where his ship had grounded and broken up, a lone malibu rider was now paddling out to try the left-hander that was breaking perhaps every six to eight minutes. Pretty slim pickings. Along the beach behind me three figures had settled for the speed of the beachbreak.

Waves? What do any of us really know?

In 1872 the clipper ship *Loch Vennacher*, on passage from Glasgow to Melbourne, on almost the same latitude as I now stood but further west, encountered two huge seas. The first one she rode over, the second one towered over the boat and broke halfway up the masts, filling the lower topsails, which were 60 feet (18 metres) above the deck.

Hundreds of tonnes of water swept over the ship, taking out its masts and washing the cook and his galley overboard. So violent was the shock and so loud the shrieking of the wind, that none of the crew, who were clinging to the poop deck, heard the crash of the breaking rigging as the masts came down.

In 1933 in the north Pacific, the American naval vessel USS *Ramapo* rode out a typhoon during which she encountered a wave of 110 feet (34 metres).

What do any of us really know? A bridgehead of sorts, a frontier if you like, has been put down with towed-in surfing, but there's still a lot of virgin territory to be explored.

GENESIS

There is no real beginning to the process. It never started at a known date. Its origins are obscure, a mishmash of myth and scientific hyperbole. But somewhere in the aeons of time, in the swirling of dust and cloud, a process was begun that has gone on for millions of years.

The component parts are many. The variables and combinations almost defy mathematical analysis. Hot air rises, cool air descends. The tilt and rotation of the earth and its orbit of the sun give rise to higher temperatures at the equator than the poles and a massive circulation of sorts begins.

A movement of air is deflected, pushed and drawn this way and that by the earth's geography, by pressure and temperature differences, hemispheres, solar flares, the heating of deserts and oceans, the heights and alignments of mountain ranges, coastlines and the all pervasive spin of the earth, what has been called the Coriolis effect which 'bends' the wind.

Westerly belts, subtropical convergences, jet streams, warm and cold fronts, cyclone and anti-cyclone, the list goes on. But eventually it all relates to wind energy and open ocean swell.

In 1643 Evangilista Torricelli invented an instrument to measure atmospheric pressure — what in time became the barometer.

In 1816, using Torricelli's invention, H.W. Brandes of the University of Breslau drew the first known isobaric weather chart and confirmed that weather sequences corresponded with giant atmospheric circulations of high and low pressures that moved around the earth.

The *Sydney Morning Herald* of 5 February 1877 published Australia's first weather map. It featured among its detail a low over southern New South Wales that was moving eastwards. I've sometimes wondered what was the effect of that as it moved out to sea.

In all this release of energy and its ocean potential, the one horrifying figure that stands like a beacon in my mind is the 347 kilometre per hour winds generated in the Gulf of Mexico in 1969 by Hurricane Camille.

I have often heard surfing described as a 'weather sensitive' activity.

OFF THE WIND

Of the thirty thousand inhabitants on the Gilbert Islands in my time, less than twenty could speak with authority about the stars, and those who had the authority were often unwilling to pass it on, for of all the secrets, those connected with navigation were the most jealously guarded.

Arthur Grimble : *Early Writings*

We had finally left the river mid-morning on a Friday, after two days holed up waiting for the nor'wester to ease off. When we awoke that morning the wind was still shrieking through the masts of the fishing boats and one of the fishermen, a character they called 'Slippery', said to me by way of warning when he knew we were leaving, 'Nothing fine ever came out of the northwest.'

The fishermen had stood on their boats watching as we motored upstream to turn around. Not one of them said a word. They stood there silently surrounded by their craypots and ropes and plastic floats and it was obvious what they thought.

At the river mouth I looked across to where the lighthouse stood starkly etched white against the grey of the cloudbank to the south. A genuine ten-foot swell was sweeping round the point and peeling down the reef, its top being torn back by the wind. Not a surfer was out.

We hoisted a heavily reefed mainsail and a tiny jib, and set off at breakneck speed down the coast. At that stage the slant of the wind was still offshore, but as we pulled out from under the headland that sheltered the river mouth we began lifting to what the met. bureau was calling a 'heavy swell'. The land to the north was partially obscured by rain squalls and appeared only at times as the drifts scudded through. At that stage the wind was probably around 30 knots with higher squalls.

The midday forecast was for gale warnings, grazier and sheep weather alerts and a litany of other diabolical weather extremes. None of us said anything when we heard it. We were only thankful we were going with it. The barometer, which had been falling for nearly twenty-four hours, continued downwards.

In the early afternoon of that initial day, the first of the cold fronts swept in from the southwest just as Slippery had intimated they would. We gybed across to take the new slant it offered, but such was the force of the wind and the size of the swell that quickly built up with it, that even with the mainsail let out the boat heeled so much that the boom dragged dangerously in the water. We brought it in, dropped the sail and ran off under the jib alone. God, it was bleak.

By nightfall as we passed the Cape and headed out to sea, a huge open ocean swell had made in, hailstones the size of fingernails were hitting the deck, the sea was a heaving mess of blown spume and an albatross was calmly criss-crossing our wake.

In the early part of the night successive fronts swept across us. We steered by the feel of the wind over our right shoulders and the direction of the swell.

Around midnight the wind steadied to a constant 30 knots with gusts to 45 or 50, which is what it had been blowing for periods of the afternoon. A full moon would occasionally break through the cloud drift, illuminating the whole tumbling madness in a veil of ghostly white.

Standing at the wheel with 55 feet (17 metres) of yacht stretched out there in front of me, the jib rock solid with wind, the whole scene took on a surreal, dreamlike air, an unreality not unlike a video game.

The most unbelievable swells were passing under us. Sometimes their tops were breaking just 'over there' in great thundering, rolling cascades of white water. Occasionally the noise would be astern and come down over us, hitting the yacht with a thump, sending up plumes of spray and filling the cockpit, leaving you gripping the wheel thigh-deep in water.

At other times the stern would slowly lift as the swell swept in, the yacht would rise, then at the top its bow would dip slowly further and further down, until the whole 12 tonnes of boat would begin a headlong rush at 18 knots down into the moonlit valley below. Surfing? I found out about surfing that night.

I thought of William Albert Robinson, a maritime wanderer and seeker of truth, and what he described as 'the culminating experience of a lifetime of voyaging'. Deep in the great southern sea his 70-foot (21-metres) and 50-tonne yacht *Varua* had slid down the faces of huge concave seas like a surfboard. 'When you have done that,' Robinson wrote, 'you have experienced something.'

Our course took us out even deeper into the ocean and eventually northeastwards towards what had been called 'Pacifica'.

For us at that time it was still a myth of sorts, a concept, if you like. The opening of Tavarua and the surf camps of the Pacific hadn't really touched us. In a sense we were still innocents and our trip had connotations of Melville and Stevenson, Jack London and Louis Becke. Not one of us gave a hoot about Kelly Slater or anyone else. Sure, they were surfers, but so were we.

The gale of the first night passed and in retrospect was the hardest weather of our passage. If you have to cop these things then the best that can happen to you is that they pick you up early and that you're going the same way as they are. Over the entire duration of our passage we experienced a weather spectrum from gale to calm.

Each morning the sun would rise almost dead ahead, lifting from the sea as a bright golden orb on some, while on others its energy and radiance would be hidden behind cloudbanks from which shafts of light shot upwards and outwards.

At times we used natural phenomena to guide us. Swell and wind directions, cloud formations, birdlife at sea and of course always the stars. For nights on end we would pick up a rising star, hold it for some hours against a known point of the rigging, such as a crosstree or shroud, and then as it rose higher in its eternal traverse of the sky we'd move to another lower star and repeat the process. In this way we might start the night with Altair fine off the bow and finish it with Betelgeuse held on the starboard crosstree. Tahitians call this star path, or succession of rising and setting stars down which you steer the *Aveia*; Tongans call it the *Kaveinga*.

With our sextants and charts and tables and satellite navigation, of course we were dilettantes, players in the great sweep of voyaging. Our destination lay out there some place with a set of known co-ordinates. Not for us the great unknown. After five days in the open ocean with no land, just 'the blue desert', I remembered the reaction of Caroline Islanders when first shown a magnetic compass by sixteenth-century Spanish explorers. When he realised the function of the compass, one of the Islanders pointed to a grey-haired old man standing on the beach and indicated that inside *his* head was *their* compass.

Whales, sharks, dolphins and seabirds crossed our tracks periodically. In the dark of night sometimes dolphins would streak towards us like torpedoes, trailing great tails of luminescence behind them. On the third morning a humpback whale surfaced beside us barely ten metres away, and stayed there following us for the best part of an hour. His hide was scarred in long streaks with barnacles encrusted in lumps here and there.

The days and nights passed. The continuous motion of the boat at sea became our world, its slow progress the measure of our time. Our lives eventually left the land, severing to some extent even the emotional idea of land and home. Our universe was the yacht and the sea and sky around us. Food and sleep came to assume immense importance for each of us, and in this way we rolled from day into night into day, from one watch to another, from gale to calm, sunlight to rain, swell to swell.

Early on the morning of the tenth day, sometime around 2 a.m., as I peered above the spray dodger to check the sea ahead, I caught the first smell of land. Perhaps it was pine needles, or grass, or just earth, but the aroma clearly caught my nostrils. It might not have been the scent of vanilla and musk that first greeted Conrad or Stevenson, but the effect was the same for me. It meant we were no longer alone out there, but more than that, for me it was another landfall at dawn.

We sighted the island soon after first light. A small indistinct dot in the grey haze of the horizon. As we worked our way in closer, its features took definition — mountains, valleys, palm trees, a lighthouse and habitation.

Just before midday we passed through the opening in the reef of the atoll west of the lighthouse. It was low tide and on either side the reef lay dried out and exposed. Off into the far distance here and there lay a series of rusting broken hulks, fishing boats, yachts and island traders that had somehow missed the entrance and ploughed up onto the coral.

As we passed through the reef, the outgoing tide created a turbulence and where it met the brunt of the open ocean swells it caused them to stand up and the odd one was close to feathering. On either side of us, stretching off to left and right as far as the eye could see, eight- to ten-foot flawlessly formed waves were peeling left and right and running uninterruptedly for hundreds of metres. There was no one out, there was no surf camp, and we were the only surfers there that I knew of.

Standing on the deck slowly making our way in past all this I heard someone use the phrase 'the frontier of surfing'. It was where we had arrived all right, but I wasn't too sure just then if that's the exact term I'd have used.

EPIPHANY

It was a warm summer's evening and the Arno valley lay stretched out below us. Heapings of rain clouds hung heavily on the hills in the distance, offering a rare evening respite from the humidity of the day.

We were on an escarpment of some sort, and behind us a cobbled walkway fell steeply away to the main street of Fiesole. Pencil pines and old villas reached away in clusters along the ridgelines to our left and right. Directly under us a copse of olive trees clung to the slope that stretched down at an oblique angle to the countryside below.

The heat of the day had lost its edge and as the sun dropped a light breeze lifted the haze and pollution of Florence so that the city, with its domes and spires and bridges and acres of red tiles, took on a clearer definition. For a time, here and there in the far distance below us, a window or a surface of some type would catch the golden light of the setting sun and send it back as a pinpoint of vibrant, intense luminescence.

As the day finally settled and drew itself off the earth as a handkerchief is drawn from the pocket, a soft purple darkness slipped in to take its place. Slowly lights became visible spreading through the valley in clusters and lines in all directions, until they glinted like a million dollars as far as the eye could see.

We were seated on a stone wall looking down on all this. There were four of us — Giannino, Annmaree, Laurene and myself. By one of those quirks of fate, or Karma, it was surfing that had brought me here, and the incongruity of it all was not lost on me.

Earlier that morning I had experienced one of my life's most profound moments. Jet-lagged and footsore I had stumbled into the Basilica of Santa Croce, a Franciscan church dating from the second half of the thirteenth century. Surrounded by 600-year-old frescoes and the tombs of Renaissance figures such as Michelangelo and Machiavelli, I found myself in a small alcove to the lower left of the main altar.

A cluster of candles burned before a statue of the Virgin. Who had lit each one of these, I wondered, and for what hopes did those flames flicker? From the corner of my right eye a movement caused me to half turn. There, in the gloom and grey of the vault that reached above the main altar, a single shaft of light hit a gold-embossed crucifix suspended perhaps four metres above the ground. In that precise instant, for the first time in my life, I understood with great clarity the basis of my own religious impulse, its relationship to the great sweep of human endeavour, and my long and fruitless search for peace, with its metaphor of the perfect wave.

Now, in the warm embrace of the night air, seated on a stone wall outside Fiesole, with its Etruscan tombs and amphitheatres, hundreds of kilometres from a wave of any sort, I faced again 'the frontier of surfing'.

Ostensibly, we were talking about surf fashion, which is what had indirectly brought me to Florence, and its relationship to surfing itself. Giannino, who had never surfed in his life, used the term 'the *idea* of surfing' in describing how it was the activity itself blurred at the edges and became something far bigger into which all people could reach for whatever it was they sought.

At one point I suddenly discovered we were discussing a memory of a group of Australian surfers and their DFA: the 'Dance of the Flaming Arseholes'. The discordance between the story and the surroundings didn't seem to matter. In fact, it was better than that, they went together like whisky and water. Culture, time and geography didn't amount to a hill of beans.

During all this, Annmaree, who told the DFA story, in another context made mention of a 'frontier of surfing'. I thought of how that phrase had come to me on a beach in Torquay, on the deck of a yacht in the western Pacific and now on a hillside above Florence.

In their own ways each of them captures something of the moveable feast that surfing is for me; the fact that it travels through time and place, from a wind blowing over the open ocean imparting its wave energy, to the deepest recesses of a mind pondering a shaft of light and a crucifix in a Florentine cathederal, or a piece of glass washed up on a beach.

When we left the hillside and made our way down the cobbled walkway to a restaurant with a vine-covered terrace, the frontier came with me, just as it always will. We dined on bean soup and drank Chianti. In the upper reaches of the Arno valley, somewhere out there in the night, a perfect wave stood up, feathered, then peeled off flawlessly along the edges of my mind.

Acknowledgments

Over a long period of time many people have helped me in various ways with these stories.

One group helped me in the writing and publishing of them, and included: Tim Baker, Ted Bainbridge, John Best, Fiona Capp, Bruce Channon, Robert Debelle, Alex Dick-Read, Jon Frank, Andrew Kidman, Wayne Lynch, Hugh McLeod, Tony Murrell, Keith Platt and Mick Sowry.

Another group supported me by their friendship and encouragement of my surf writing. This group included: Craig 'Gonzo' Baird, David Bouchier, Simon Buttonshaw, Chris Carey, Keith Curtain, Chris Dance, Brad Gerlach, Russell Graham, Ross Harrison, Annmaree Kealy, Barry 'Tubes' Langan, Ross Lindsay, Russell McConachy, Jason O'Loughlin, Doug Rogers, and Craig Stevenson.

At various times over almost thirty years I have exchanged punches, kicks, and observations on life with Simon Buttonshaw. His thoughts have always been important to me, their origins invariably from well down the road less travelled, their articulation precise and cerebral. I am grateful for his Foreword to this book, with its incisive comments on surfing, life, and the perspectives of the stories themselves.

Jon Frank was with this project from the moment it first left the beach and paddled out to an uncertain lineup. He is without doubt one of surfing's foremost photo artists, and to have his work alonside my stories has been an outcome of grace and immense good fortune.

I owe Alison Urquhart and Jennifer Blau, my publisher and editor at HarperCollins, a huge debt of thanks for their belief in this project, and their professionalism in its execution.

I am deeply grateful to all of these people, and to countless unnamed others, who have helped me ride waves and then try to write about it. I hope the torch of what might be loosely called 'surf literature', continues to be picked up and taken forward by younger writers. The subject certainly deserves it!

Jack Finlay

WAVES
GREAT STORIES FROM THE SURF

Tim Baker
General Editor

Tim Winton • Phil Jarratt • Sean Doherty
Fiona Capp • DC Green • Matt Griggs • Tim Baker • Nick Carroll
Pam Burridge • Andrew Kidman • Jack Finlay • Jimmy O'Keefe • Mark Warren

Waves: Great Stories from the Surf

This collection of great Australian surf stories sheds new light on the 'moveable feast' that is modern surfing, and gives an intimate insider's view of the mad compulsion to ride waves — whatever the costs.

If you've never surfed, these stories will make you want to start. If you already surf, they'll remind you why you're never going to stop . . .

MP: the life of Michael Peterson

Michael Peterson makes *Fear and Loathing in Las Vegas* look like *Alice in Wonderland*.

For three years Michael Peterson was the best surfer in the world, hands down.

The gangly, long-haired rebel from Coolangatta breathed saltwater, and ruled the waves with savage, groundbreaking surfing. The guy was worshipped like a god — other surfers simply got out of the water to watch him, and girls threw themselves at him. But once you discover his dark beginnings, you'll understand why 'MP' was destined never to be your average guy. Michael Peterson was a tortured genius . . . and one complex cat.

An undiagnosed schizophrenic, Michael despised the fame his surfing powers attracted, and he retreated into a world of hard drugs, fast cars and shadows. He eventually hit rock bottom after a car chase, which took thirty-five police cars to stop him. After years of jail and psychiatric institutions he emerged, alive, but bearing the scars of his battle.

For twenty years Michael Peterson's exploits in and out of the water have existed only as a series of mythological tales, passed down by the surfing tribe. Until now.

Bustin' Down the Door

From street urchin to world surfing champion to boardroom heavyweight, this new and revised edition of the bestselling cult classic captures all the intrigue and adventure of Wayne 'Rabbit' Bartholomew's remarkable personal journey.

World Champion in 1978, World Masters Champion in 1999, and currently CEO/President of the Association of Surfing Professionals, Rabbit's charisma, flamboyance and warrior spirit have helped define surfing over three decades.

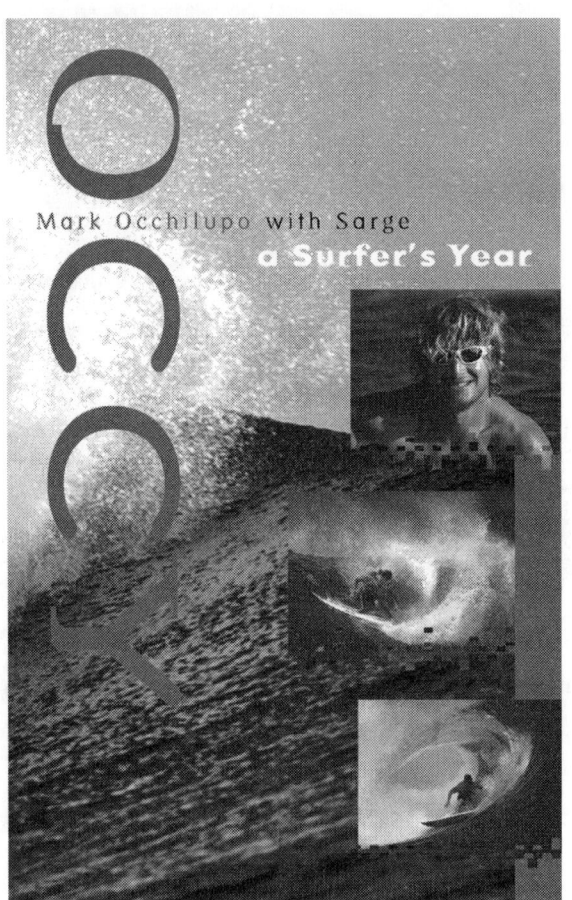

Occy: A Surfer's Year

The surfing diary of the year by World Champion Mark Occhilupo's as he travels the world: Fiji, South Africa, the tournament at Bells and more. This, his on-the-road diary, gives us an insight into the mind of one of Australia's cult sport heroes. It provides a rare opportunity to go with Occy as he defends his crown — the diary documents his observations on other surfers, his tournaments, mindset and life on the road.